The Problem of Perversion

The Problem of Perversion

The View from Self Psychology

Arnold Goldberg, M.D.

Yale University Press
New Haven and London

Designed by Sally Harris, Summer Hill Books.
Set in Melior type by The Composing Room of Michigan, Inc.
Printed in the United States of America by Vail-Ballou Press, Binghamton, New York.

Library of Congress Cataloging-in-Publication Data

Goldberg, Arnold, 1929–
    The problem of perversion : the view from self psychology / Arnold Goldberg.
        p.   cm.
    Includes bibliographical references and index.
    ISBN 0-300-06030-0 (cl : alk. paper)

    1. Sexual deviation.   2. Self psychology.   3. Psychosexual disorders.   I. Title.
    [DNLM: 1. Psychosexual Disorders—psychology.   2. Psychosexual Disorders—therapy.   3. Self Concept.   4. Psychoanalytic Interpretation.   WM 190 G618p 1995]
    RC556.G65   1995
    616.85'83—dc20
    DNLM/DLC
    for Library of Congress   94-28556
                                                                           CIP

10 9 8 7 6 5 4 3 2 1

To Andrew and Sarah

Contents

vii

Acknowledgments

I am especially grateful not only to my friend and teacher, Heinz Kohut, whose work this book hopes to enlarge upon, but also to Robert Stoller, whom I never met but who was clearly a trailblazer in this field. A group of friends—Mark Gehrie, Brenda Solomon, David Solomon, and Jeffrey Stern—read and criticized an early draft of the book and made many helpful comments. Otto Kernberg introduced my to Yale University Press and Gladys Topkis, whose editing was both helpful and encouraging. My manuscript was made more readable by the combined efforts of that exceptional staff, including Lorraine Alexson and Dan Heaton.

Portions of Chapter 3 appeared in the *Psychoanalytic Quarterly* and of Chapter 4 in *A Fresh Look at Psychoanalysis*, published by Analytic Press. Finally, I am in need of yet another editor to fully express my unending appreciation and thanks to Christine Susman, who typed, retyped, arranged, corrected, and did more things than I could ever imagine to see this to completion.

Introduction

Perversion is a problem. Initially, it is such because it defies concise and clear definition. Since one man's or woman's personal choice may be another's anathema, we are often unable definitively to distinguish preference from pathology. But perversion is also a problem because we seem unable to treat it effectively even when we are able to pin it down as pathological. Thus, the task before us is both to define it and, once having qualified it as an illness, to treat it. As I shall show, the task is partly accomplished by attending less to the behavior and more to the psychological forces that lie behind it. What looks normal may not be so, and to delve into what seems abnormal may make it less so.

In this book I elaborate on concepts of psychoanalytic self psychology with the particular aim of better explaining, interpreting, and ultimately understanding perverse behavior. The idea for the work originated in a number of suggestions offered by the late Heinz Kohut about the problem of perversion and how a self psychological perspective might yield a solution. What seemed, sadly, to be the fate of self psychology in the post-Kohut era was that it led to a series of works that primarily reiterated the same ideas or various applications of the same limited scope without much effort to develop the work along the lines Kohut had suggested. The difficulties of such a project more than explain its lack of realization. I have found myself rediscovering ideas that I have read in Kohut, and thus I, too, may be guilty of redescription in my own effort to achieve originality.

Regardless of whether or not my ideas are new, it is worthwhile to call attention once again to this spectrum of disorders, which I believe remains unyielding to psychoanalytic and psychotherapeutic techniques when they fail to include the contributions of psychoanalytic self psychology. That the disorders of perversion are indeed responsive to this different orientation is a promissory note for anyone who chooses to pursue the study and the technique. One cannot, of course, realistically extend a debate about these issues until and unless mutual understanding has been reached. Self psychology as an extension of psychoanalysis contributes to our definition because it helps us, on the one hand, to see perverse behavior as an aid in self-cohesion and, on the other, to see it as a pathological condition in terms of its exploitation of other persons.

I therefore start with a definition composed of three essential components: sexualization, splitting, and a specific set of psychodynamics. It may seem to some an easy task to say what a perversion is, as defining pornography was for a noted Supreme Court justice: "I know it when I see it." It turns out, however, that the definition is not so simple, because we fall readily into the gap between a definition by description and one achieved by more scientific scrutiny, involving subjective experience, a hallmark of self psychology. Although sexual behavior may appear and be described as normal or perverse, it begins to qualify as perverse only when it causes discomfort or pain to the participants and represents what the scientific community deems pathological. That sort of definition by authority enables an investigator to lift perversion out of a network involving civil rights and liberties and place it in an arena framed by psychoanalytic ideas about normal and deviant actions. So, like it or not, psychoanalysis defines perversion by psychoanalytic standards of normality and so removes it from the area of common sense or folk psychology; that is, it is not a matter of opinion.

I posit the problem of perversion as one of psychological structure. There is no doubt that this focus itself gives rise to many problems, which can be summed up in a now familiar either-or position: structural conflict versus structural deficit. Because there can be no manifest conflict without a corresponding structural deficit, and vice versa, this controversy is really a nonissue. Every conflict we know of through a negative emotional experience or symptom must have resulted from a developmental failure that prevented satisfactory resolution of the conflict. If we put aside issues that are conscious matters of indecision (whether to wear this hat or another), as we should, we can focus on a psychic conflict involving an unconscious wish, fantasy, or memory that has not been put to rest and is thus expressed not as an integrated product of a functioning self, but rather as a member of an unhappy psychological household—that is, it is painful or troublesome or makes optimal functioning difficult. All such problems result from a structural failure of some sort. So, too, do all deficiencies in the psyche necessarily lead to problems; otherwise they would be assets rather than deficiencies. The neatness of the "no conflict without a deficit" situation becomes a problem only if and when we aim to spell out particulars—what type of defect leads to or involves what type of conflict, and vice versa. Yet to assume the possibility of structural integrity along with a neurotic symptom is to ask how cure by insight could possibly take place. Knowledge itself is not enough. Essentially, structural theoretical concepts such as neutralization or ego strength must be invoked; that is, any neurotic symptom reflects a structural weakness or failure at some level, and treatment must somehow alter that state. Successful treatment results certainly suggest structural change and a deficiency as their precursors. Similarly, we posit a variety of structural defects as being responsible for all manner of conflicts. What is needed, obviously, is a better matching of deficit and conflict, a better explanation of why a conflict is expressed in a certain way rather than another. This is the stance of a true structural psychology and psychopathology that expands the boundaries of the vast group called ego weaknesses, or self deficits. Clearly, a deficit is more than a missing piece, and a weakness is more than diminished strength. This book is therefore an effort to discuss those structural problems of the self that seem to be prevalent in perversion. I will amplify my threefold definition as I describe the nature of the structure in detail, that is, the self along with the specifics of the structural deficit.

I hope this work will also be seen as an effort to expand upon the personal vision presented in my earlier work (with John Gedo), *Models of the Mind* (1971). That book essentially viewed the psychoanalytic enterprise through the use of various theoretical models. Such pluralism, we argued, is required of all practitioners because, wittingly or unwittingly, we do a variety of things to and with patients, some of which contribute to the hoped-for benefit of the treatment. It is vital that we know as much as we can about how we affect patients, from pacification to the gaining of insight. At no time, however, was the message of *Models of the Mind* meant to be prescriptive, since that would make us educators or trainers rather than therapists or analysts. Our activity should singularly be that of interpretation, with a clear recognition that the prerequisite for a gain from this activity is, for many patients, a period in which the interpretations are seemingly without effect. However one may conceptualize this period, as a holding environment or an understanding phase, interpretation is the sine qua non of analysis. Without that limiting framework we are embarked on a voyage of possibly unlimited license of interaction between patient and analyst. I have no doubt that many efforts are needed to repair damaged and perhaps undeveloped selves (Basch 1988 is the clearest exponent of such efforts). Still, an analysis that aims at wholesale self-reorganization cannot reach its goal without the self-reflective quality that derives only from interpretation (Goldberg 1988). And, of course, we have long ago discarded the idea of interpretation as the uncovering of hidden meanings (the archaeological model) and now recognize that every interpretation is a construction and creator of new meanings.

The study of perverse behavior soon takes on a double standard because of its situation in the world. Although one may wish to isolate a particular action such as fetishism and consider it relevant only to an individual person's performance, that can never be done, because context is a necessary determinant of perverse behavior, and no one pursues a perversion oblivious to that context. The existence of the action therefore must be seen as dependent upon its position in the world. We are better able to comprehend just how one manages to be both in the real world while behaving as if in another, unreal world by understanding the fundamental contribution of splitting. Regardless of the tortured journey of this concept in the psychoanalytic vocabulary, from denial to disavowal to vertical splitting, it is an opening to a potential revolution in psychoanalytic theory. I am convinced that many psychological subjects require restudy on the basis of this concept. For example, the heated debate about insanity—knowing right from wrong—becomes a totally different problem when we see that conflicting personalities may seem to coexist in a nonintegrated self: one can do horrendous things in one sector of a self while another sector, which surely knows right from wrong, is temporarily stilled. In this book I consider the concept of splitting primarily on the basis of perverse action residing in the split-off part of the self. The range of reactions of its parallel partner becomes a crucial element of our capacity to understand and treat the aberrant behavior.

The psychopathology of the self is sometimes presented as a disorder of self-development, proceeding along the single axis of narcissism. The crucial developmental step required to differentiate borderline and psychotic disorders from narcissistic personality and behavior disorders is the formation of a cohesive self. This psychic structure in the routine story of self psychology became the linchpin for the study of the self and its sustaining selfobject, and thus pathology became focused on self-fragmentation and the resultant products of self-disintegration. The picture of pathology therefore tended to have a single and simple line—fragmentation or cohesion: viewed along this continuum, the self is either intact or it is falling apart. Historical emphasis soon gave way to a call for more careful and detailed delineations of self disorders, such as those that did not demonstrate fragmentation but clearly showed other signs of psychic pain. Predominant in this group was the self of empty depression, or the depleted self, and the forms of behavior employed to counteract the anguish of that feeling of hollowness. Perverse behavior is commonly used in this effort, and I examine two cases of a sexualization in the form of lovesickness, or erotomania. Each case demonstrates the sexualization, vertical split, and special dynamics associated with the disorder and thus fulfills the requirements of my definition of perversion, one comprising three crucial elements that singly cannot make for perversion.

No discussion of perverse behavior can avoid dealing with the political problems that smolder around the topic, particularly as regards homosexuality and its relation to psychopathology. In this book I consider all sexual behavior as potentially pathological, including heterosexual intercourse, so as to study its role in the overall functioning of the self. Since many forms of behavior are not allowed membership in the community of the normal— that is, although the borders may shift, some perversions are never admitted—we cannot equally rank any and all sexual behaviors as potentially normal. Yet, surely all perversions have a psychology that can be studied and understood, and we should try to do so before considering how a behavior may become part of the total functioning of the self. With that in mind, I have sought to isolate one way in which homosexual behavior can come about—that is, through its psychology. I then consider homosexuality both as a manifestation of psychopathology and in a form that leads to a well-functioning self. In looking at homosexuality as a compensatory structure, I do not intend to refer to all homosexuality, to indicate that this behavior is necessarily either pathological or healthy, or to suggest that it be treated as a disorder. My intention is to understand the psychology of some homosexuals better and, more important, to illustrate significant limitations in our therapeutic interventions. Along with splitting, hostility is a psychological phenomenon equally in need of study and comprehension in cases of perversion. It is an almost universally agreed-upon component of perversion, one that for many scholars occupies center stage in the study of sexual dysfunction. The associated rage and anger seen in cases of perversion, ranging from rape to consensual sadomasochistic acts, demand explanation, often revolving around the simplistic answer that sex is the secondary element and hostility the primary one. The callous disregard of the sexual partner's feelings in many forms of perversion, as well as forms that seem primarily directed at expressing anger and inflicting pain and injury, would support this answer. I suspect, however, that answer to be in error. Addressing the anger instead of the sex seems no more likely to reveal a solution. Suffice it to say that self psychologists do not view anger as most psychoanalysts do. The first step is instead to differentiate normal aggression from reactive rage in order better to position the prevalence of rage and hostility in a specific perversion as a fundamental narcissistic disorder. Thus we consider a form of narcissistic pathology to be the underlying explanation for the outbursts of rage that often accompany perverse behavior.

No one could possibly do justice to the treatment of disorders of perverse behavior in a single chapter. Rather, I highlight the salient problems involved in treatment and position the disorders as eminently analyzable. I must emphasize the status of psychoanalysis in this regard, in particular psychoanalytic self psychology. Although I doubt that weekly or twice-weekly psychotherapy can ameliorate perverse behavior, I certainly acknowledge that almost all perverse behavior may diminish or cease during therapy of almost any kind. The biggest problem in all treatments is the recurrence of the symptom after therapy. In the few cases I report on here, there has been long-term follow-up. All the case vignettes are disguised. Many are cases I supervised, and no single dream or incident is a verbatim record. One must navigate carefully to ensure both scientific legitimacy and respect for patient privacy, and I trust that the alterations made to protect the latter have not compromised faithfulness to the former.

The important ingredient of my chapter on treatment is the widened scope of the concept of interpretation—in going beyond the lifting of repression to a state that allows a new construction, that of a unified self. A lack of unification must be seen as the failure of normal development that was a solution of sorts for the patient, and so it will be maintained as a solution over severe resistances. For the person who operates with two sets of ambitions, goals, and values, it is no easy task to eradicate one or to absorb one into the other. In many such persons the perverse sector becomes a method of handling emotional issues and is rarely confined to the occasional or sporadic outburst that may have characterized its origin. The perverse sector may indeed become an equal member of the person's psychological self, and its full disappearance is more than many people can be expected to attain. Therefore the chapter on treatment must be seen as a modest indicator of the hope for future studies in this direction, which will clarify which cases of perverse behavior are readily treatable as well as what should be a reasonable goal of such treatment.

Jacques Derrida, the founder of deconstruction, calls his pursuit a dismantling (Sarup 1993). This viewpoint appropriately characterizes my final chapter, which looks at perversion from different perspectives in order to "unpack" the many meanings of the term, to go beyond the behavior to the person. I use the words *explanation, interpretation, meaning,* and *understanding* in this project of taking perversion apart. I think it has to be approached in this manner because it is not an affliction in the way an infectious disease is, which can come upon a person suddenly and perhaps just as easily leave. Perversions are an integral part of the total composition of a person, and when we evaluate such a person we must be able to see the structure that constitutes the perverse behavior. The proper view of perversion neither espouses trying to control it nor hopes for its disappearance. Both approaches would treat perversion as a foreign intrusion in the person and would thereby risk bypassing the person and therefore forgo understanding. Explaining perversion will help us to see what causes it; interpreting perversion is the way psychoanalysts try to make sense of it. The meaning of perversion is its place in the world, and understanding it is the way we connect to the person. Such a connection is an empathic link that becomes part and parcel of that self-cohesion that is a prerequisite of successful functioning. If we explain perversion we get to the roots of its beginning. When we interpret perversion we see it as standing in for something else. As we position perversion in the world we see what it means to us. But only when we understand the person with perverse behavior are we able to aid in its amelioration, to solve the problem. Together these four words allow us to unlock the puzzle, and so we start.

1

A New Definition of Perversion

It is well to begin with Webster, which tells us that the perverse is that which is turned away from the right and the good and is therefore incorrect and improper. A perversion is a perverted form of something, especially "that form of sexual gratification preferred to heterosexual coitus and habitually sought after as the primary or only form of sex gratification desired." This definition, however, demands that we both know what is right and good and agree that heterosexual coitus enjoys that rank among us all—except the perverse. The definition therefore assumes a guide to the agreed-upon societal considerations of correct behavior, especially sexual behavior, and the psychological norm for such behavior. We know that community sanctions and license have much to do with whether one or another form of sexual behavior is tolerated or encouraged. We also know that psychoanalysis, for example, has postulated a normal line of sexual development that begins with certain zones or areas of pleasure and culminates in a zone of genital and therefore heterosexual gratification. Psychoanalysis makes the claim that it essentially knows what is right and normal and so can clearly say what is a perversion and what is not.

I propose to fashion a psychoanalytic definition with three components: the individual psychodynamics of the person, the split in his or her sense of reality, and the use of sexualization. I discuss and evaluate each of these elements in detail to form a new definition of perversion.

Psychoanalysis Searches for a Definition

In psychoanalysis, perversion is a path of deviant or wayward behavior. That picture, however, does not coincide with a social climate of permissiveness and a wide range of pleasure-seeking activity. For Anna Freud (1965), the diagnosis of perversion in an adult signifies that the primacy of the genitals was never established or was not maintained; that is, that in the sexual act itself the pregenital components were not reduced to an introductory or contributing role, as they are in normal development. Perversions, therefore, are a form of developmental failure. Earlier, Sigmund Freud (1905) defined perversion as sexual activities that either extend, in an anatomical sense, beyond the regions of the body designed for sexual union or linger on the intermediate relations to the sexual object. Thus, perversions are wayward and lost. Those who engage in perverse activity are indulging in forms of gratification that should be discarded or become secondary. To Freud, this particular form of indulgence allowed one to escape neurosis, for true neurotics cannot allow themselves to express perverse impulses. This neat but probably simplistic definition allowed Freud to claim that there is a reciprocal relation between neurosis and perversion, so that one could have one or the other but not both, although both were clearly related to the Oedipus complex: neurosis as a compromise symptom; perversion as an escape. While neurosis bans the impulse, perversion gives it license.

   Edward Glover (1932) decided that the view of a perversion as an escape from the oedipal phase was unsatisfactory and perhaps incomplete. He felt that the most profitable way to understand perversions was by organizing them along the line of development of the reality sense—psychological contact with the object or person, or, more simply, seeing another realistically. He felt that perversions show an orderly series of differentiations in both aim and completeness of the object, but that this developmental order runs parallel to that of psychoses, transitional states, or what today might be considered borderline syndromes, neuroses, and social inhibitions. He suggested that perversions assist in preserving the amount of reality sense already achieved, by what becomes a sacrifice of freedom in one's adult libidinal function. Thus perversion for Glover was said to be correlated with one's sense of reality, and he gave us more of a promissory note for a fuller explanation than a clear-cut categorization. Glover postulated a developmental series of anxiety situations that could give rise to either neurotic symptom formation or perversion formation. Perversions, he argued, patched over flaws in the development of the reality sense and could be found in association with a fairly normal ego or with definite forms of psychosis. He assumed that perversions not only preserve one's reality testing (the capacity to retain psychic contact with objects), but "indicate the order in which reality sense develops" (p. 226). Glover felt that a careful study of the subdivisions of the oral and other erotogenic zones would disclose an order that would reveal the development of reality. He himself never did such a study, and his hope of better connecting reality and perverse behavior has not been realized.

Glover thereupon added another dimension to the definition of perversion; it now consisted of a wayward drive plus a blindness or at least diminished or flawed vision. Glover was guided in his pursuit of the problem of reality by Freud's famous article on fetishism (1927). In that essay Freud established the foundation for all future psychoanalytic work on the perversions, and it is there that he presented the idea of the splitting of the ego. He claimed that this split was the prerequisite of the psyche of the perverse. That is, the ego was rent in two: one part believed one bit of reality, and the other part or segment could ignore it. This was the defense of disavowal, which for Freud followed the little boy's inevitable and fateful observation that women do not have a penis. At first this perception is not acknowledged by the boy, but with the gradual evolving of the reality ego, a new solution is necessitated, and a split, or a division, is called for. For some children a solution is available in fantasy, but others turn to a deviant sexual pattern of behavior in order to create a new reality, to circumvent the oedipal problem and the associated castration fear. Whereas the neurotic solves this dilemma by repression and symptom formation, the perverse solution is said to lie in a fundamental disavowal of sexual reality. Michael Basch (1983) explains the defense of disavowal as confined to a refusal to acknowledge the significance of what is seen. He notes that it emerges at the time of concrete operational functions, when the child can no longer maintain contraries and contradictions, and when logical thinking makes its appearance in cognitive development. This maturational step demands disavowal.

Later elaborations on the developmental line of reality (including that of Gedo and Goldberg 1974) have a certain kinship to Glover's wish to categorize this development as one moves from psychotic denial to scotoma, or focused blindness, to a disavowal of the associated affect. The "absent penis" as the prototype of an external reality that is not bearable or palatable but cannot be abolished can, however, readily be extended beyond the sexual sphere. The effort to circumscribe and define perversion as a set of dynamics and a divided ego is unfortunately weakened by the evidence that the splitting of the ego is not exclusive to sexual disorders but seems to be present in many, primarily narcissistic, psychopathologies. Kohut (1971) verticalized the concept of a split. In his vision, one part of the psyche harbored perverse activity while living apart from yet side by side with the reality ego. This vertical split was seen in all manner of disorders in which a disavowed aspect of archaic, infantile, or untamed grandiosity or idealization appeared to live in parallel with a seemingly healthy ego.

New voices have joined in linking perversion and narcissism. Joyce McDougall (1978) and Janine Chasseguet-Smirgel (1984) both claim that an act of creation occurs in perversions that allows one to effect a narcissistic reparation without the need for external intervention—that is, to make up for a narcissistic deficiency autonomously. McDougall claims that deviant sexuality is a creative effort to deal with important deficiencies stemming from the early maternal relationship, but she quickly disclaims any specificity to sexual pathology, since "narcissistic lesions" have no special claim in this regard.

Chasseguet-Smirgel pursues the concept of disavowal by adding the significance of anal regression. For her, disavowal in perversion includes the setting up of a universe or psychic arena where all differences that bring about conflict and psychic pain are abolished. This is the universe of anal-sadistic regression, wherein all elements are idealized. The anal universe rests on a reality that is filled with idealization and is realized by disavowal. It is separated, or split apart, from the real universe. The affect is not repressed but displaced, or disavowed, and so is moved from one side of the split (reality) to the other. For Chasseguet-Smirgel there is regressive analization along with both the recognition and denial of reality in regard to sexual differences. She therefore also employs the concept of a vertical split. Both she and Kohut seem to go beyond the usual attributes of the ego in their descriptions. Kohut pursues his ideas in terms of the self; Chasseguet-Smirgel at no point employs this concept, but she does expand and modify the concept of the split in order to particularize it for perversion. In doing so, she can be read as considering all perversion to be of a piece, with Freud's particular dynamics of anal regression added to the picture. Thus we continue to join the two components in a definition of perversion: the dynamics of the oedipal complex coupled with a loss or diminution in reality occasioned by a vertical split.

Robert Stoller (1975) felt that this definition was inadequate. For Stoller, the defining factor of perversion was hostility. Perversion is the result of an essential interplay between hostility and sexual desire. A perversion is the reliving of actual historical sexual trauma aimed precisely at one's sex (an anatomical state) or gender identity (masculinity or femininity), so that in the perverse act the past is rubbed out (p. 6). The source of the anger is the patient's victimization in childhood, usually by a parent or parent surrogate. Through the perversion, the anger is transformed into a victory over those who made the child wretched, for in perversion, trauma becomes triumph (p. 59).

Stoller claimed that the trauma or frustration of childhood occurred precisely at the anatomical sexual apparatus and its functions or at one's masculinity or femininity. The sexual excitement is set off at the moment when adult reality resembles the childhood trauma or frustration. The anxiety is experienced as excitement (p. 105), although how this is achieved is no clearer in Stoller's writing than anywhere else in psychoanalysis. For example, the homosexual as a child, according to Stoller, was offered the pleasure of excessive closeness by his mother, but only when, because of her bullying, he gave up his tendencies toward what the mother considered masculine behavior. His masculinity is there, preserved and disguised in effeminate-hostile mimicry (p. 155), which is a component of the perversion.

For Stoller, this form of sexual excitement is the desire to harm another, consciously or unconsciously, in order to avenge past traumas and frustrations; the sexual act serves to transform childhood trauma into adult triumph; and trauma, risk, and revenge establish a mood of excitement that is intensified when they are packaged as mystery (p. 201)—a word Stoller applied to society's attitude toward sex. Rage dispersion, for Stoller, serves to provide guilt, leading to reduced erotic pleasure; rage dispersion lowers the murder rate in families, blends into erotic pleasure, leads to an exhaustion of energies that might otherwise break society open, and deflects the hatred between the sexes (p. 218). Stoller seemed to equate all perverse activity with an expression of hostility by insisting that no matter what the act, the fantasy involved betrays a fundamental hatred. He also saw it as a safety valve for the intense rage that is ever-present in society.

That there is rage in perversions seems without question, but just how it fits into the etiology of perverse behavior is problematic. It may be profitable to determine whether the hostility in perversion is truly aimed at an object as an act of aggression or is a reaction to an injury suffered at the hands of the object, as Stoller suggests. This distinction demands that we distinguish hostility as primary or secondary. To say that the hatred present in all perversion follows from victimization and, necessarily, from a specific act of violence directed at an anatomical part is to say that it is a reactive hostility. Stoller's thinking evidences an understanding of perverse behavior limited by a constraint within classical theory. This constraint is most telling in Stoller's consideration of hostility as basic to perversion.

For some cases the sexual and hostile components of behavior cannot be distinguished from each other, as in the sphere of sadomasochistic activity. The existence of an astonishing variety of sexual behavior allows for the free play of one's imagination in divining the motives and meanings of such activity, and once embarked on an evaluation of a perverse act, one has license to explain it in any manner conceivable. Stoller (1975) put together a remarkable list of "specific indicators":

Through the act the patient acted out a confrontation of idealized and degraded images of his mother. . . . It gratified sadistic and masochistic wishes. . . . Castration anxiety and guilt were successfully warded off. . . . The perversion acted out a forbidden wish in disguised form. . . . Specifically, both the oedipal wish and the homosexual transference . . . re-enacted the primal scene. . . . It also re-enacted childhood seduction and gratification by the parents. . . . It permitted actual gratification by an actual substitute object, so that the anxiety of object loss was allayed." (p. 5)

McDougall seems to join Stoller in considering hostility as the core of perversion. She says that

perversions furnish a reply to a dual exigency: the individual, caught between his desire to exist as a separate being and the impossibility of doing so without great violence, must find in his neosexual scenario a scene of action apt to contain this violence, at the same time that he has elaborated an erotic ritual that allows sexual sharing with another. In the exchange, the subject recovers not only his self-image, but also the assurance that no one is destroyed. The latter guarantee is a cardinal element in that the fierce wish to attack the threatening object of desire is aimed, in the unconscious, at the earliest and most beloved objects. (pp. 8–9)

No stone is left unturned. Everything is explained or explainable. Clearly, we see both that the psychodynamic explanation of perversion is inadequate (or perhaps overly adequate) and that once an act becomes part of a person's repertoire, it does double duty in serving the underlying pathological origin along with other jobs. An act may then proceed to a freedom and life of its own whereby it functions according to needs far from either its psychological origin or usual form of gratification.

Completion of the Definition

Joining aspects of the dynamics suggested in perversion to the split in the ego or self falls short of a complete definition of perversion. To emphasize the hostile component or to make it the core factor of perversion not only fails to convince but makes the essence of perversion—which is and must be a variation of sexual performance—more mysterious. It is as if the eagerness to circumscribe and explain perversion has permitted a neglect of its essential component: sexualization.

The term *sexualization* begins with Freud, who explained its meaning and significance in the following quote from the Schreber case (1911):

People who have not freed themselves completely from the stage of narcissism—who, that is to say, have at that point a fixation which may operate as a disposition to a later

illness—are exposed to the danger that some unusually intense wave of libido, finding no other outlet, may lead to a
sexualization of their social instincts and so undo the sub-
limations which they had achieved in the course of their
development. The result may be produced by anything that
causes the libido to flow backward (that is, that causes a
"regression"): whether, on the one hand, the libido becomes
collaterally reinforced owing to some disappointment over
a woman, or is directly dammed up owing to a mishap in
social relations with other men—both of these being instances of "frustration"; or whether, on the other hand,
there is a general intensification of the libido, so that it becomes too powerful to find an outlet along the channels that
are already open to it, and consequently bursts through its
banks at the weakest spot. Since our analyses show that
paranoiacs endeavor to protect themselves against any such
sexualization of their social instinctual cathexes, we suppose the weak spot in their development to be looked for
somewhere between the stages of autoerotism, narcissism
and homosexuality, and that their disposition to illness
must be located in that region. (p. 62)

My reading of this text is that some relatively stable function, a
sublimation, is undone at the time of an injury and that the
resulting phenomenon is sexualization. Thus, sexual activity of
any variety, and perhaps many varieties, takes the place of or
appears following the regression of frustration or the intensification of sexuality per se. The sexual phenomena are not to be
seen, then, as solely representative of a particular conflict or a set
of dynamic forces, but rather as evidence of a structural weakness. The weakness is omnipresent in one sense but often silent
until the onset occasioned by the injury. Now the third component to the definition and construction of perversion appears:
sexualization.

Kohut, in particular, emphasized the manifestations of sexuality as an effort to substitute for narcissistically invested objects
or selfobjects or to halt the regression that follows the loss of

such objects. The developmental forms of narcissism can, in theory, express themselves in a sexualized manner, and perverse behavior may be correlated with particular stages of narcissism. Stoller postulated that sexual excitement is set off at a time when adult reality resembles childhood trauma and frustration, but Kohut, following Freud, indicated that the particulars of the reality were less important than the subsequent threat of loss of the sustaining selfobject. Some explanation must be entertained to distinguish the occasional presence or outbreak of perverse behavior from an everlasting expression of the disorder. The definition of perversion by Jean LaPlanche and Jean-Bertrand Pontalis (1973, 306) does not address the occasional presence of perversion, while Otto Kernberg adds the requirement that it be fixed and repetitive (1991).

To recapitulate: the elements of perversion are a psychodynamic statement, perhaps based on an oedipal or preoedipal theme, a split in the ego or self that allows for a disavowal of reality, and a structural vulnerability that allows for the appearance of sexualization following an injury or disappointment. I now bring the definition to a social setting to determine what behaviors qualify for the category and how the three aspects of perversion are connected to the world.

The Social Definitions of Perversion

No perversion can be lifted from the world and studied in isolation, since perversion lives in and within a network of relations. These relations are often thought of as social, but their impact is psychological, and, as I shall demonstrate, they come to form the very psyche of the individual. My definition therefore must consider the system that encompasses perverse behavior.

Stoller (1975, 3) defines aberrations as social phenomena that depart from a culture's avowed definition of normality. He then divides the category into variants and perversions. Only the latter have the quality of an acted-out fantasy and qualify as an erotic form of hatred. Whether a variant or a perversion, an aberration exists according to a cultural norm. The second demand placed on a proper definition of perversion is that it be a deviation from what is deemed normal and acceptable in a given culture.

Fritz Morgenthaler (1980), a psychoanalyst who studied sexual practices in different cultures and made many field observations (in Mali, the Ivory Coast, South America, and Madagascar), felt that Western scales and moral standards were a constraining influence on our ability to understand that a wide variety of sexual practices might be labeled perverse according to one set of mores but not according to another. He says, for instance, that in certain societies, because of their cultural and communal restrictions, psychic development suppresses the polymorphous perverse character of human sexual life, so that heterosexuality represents an "ideological monopoly of such a society's morality" (p. 130). Thus he suggests that Freud's notion of the waywardness of perverse behavior can also be seen as an implicit insistence on a single definition of correct behavior. Morgenthaler recognizes the conflictual nature of much perverse behavior but asks the analyst to be more tolerant of the potential variant paths open to people.

Morgenthaler also joins Kohut in considering perversion to be a form of narcissistic pathology, but he differs in feeling that no manifestation of a particular form of perversion can possibly be decoded according to its individualized psychological meaning outside its setting. Freud (1905) said that both internal and environmental factors bring about perversions. Yet he was unclear about the extent of external influences and certainly went no further than to indicate that the repressive forces of society and the availability of sexual objects could make for a sexual variant. If, however, we remove the criterion of "normal for a given culture at a given time," we return to a psychological definition of perversion that takes the environment into account, not so much as a standard but rather as playing a particular role in the psyche of the individual.

Imagine a person with a culturally aberrant form of sexual behavior transported to a society that sanctions that behavior. This would be the simplest evidence of the relativity of the definition of perverse, and it is probably also the rarest of events in an analyst's casebook. Once accepted, the perversion is no longer seen as a deviance. There could, however, be a subgroup in that transported population comprising those members whose perverse behavior changes, is modified, or indeed disappears in the new set of circumstances; that is, it is not a question of acceptance but of dissipation or disappearance. Of course, this is a different effect of the environment, one that is in stark contrast to the individual whose perversion is a painful and unhappy affliction without any relevance to the environment. His behavior is either not substantially relieved or relaxed by an environmental sanction or is something that hardly any society would support. Now consider a third person, one who insists on always being at odds with society, one for whom aberrance is a necessity. Thus, the so-called external or environmental factors need to be more closely joined to the issues noted earlier in my psychoanalytic assessment of perversion—the dynamics, the split, and the sexualization. Seeing the individual with perverse behavior in the world changes our way of considering the nature of perversion.

The first of the three elements that constitute a perversion—the particular dynamics involved—need not detain us long. Psychodynamics is a point of view which states that unconscious factors may lead to varieties of symptom formation. Some symptoms may be more palatable than others, but the fundamental nature of the conflict is a clash of forces that are internal. (As I will explain, this formulation does not hold true in the same sense in the narcissistic disorders.) Further, any single set of dynamics causes a problem in explaining the variability of occurrence of perverse acts: dynamics are static, while perversions are, for the most part, sporadic. The hysteric's paralyzed arm usually does not come and go (if it does, one wonders about the diagnosis). Yet perversions seem acutely tied to either the rise of sexual tension or something else in the environment. The outbreak of an otherwise hidden or even forbidden act of sexual behavior in an individual who does not usually employ it demands a different explanation from that for a long-standing, habitual form that may or may not be concealed. The first explanation would be that the act is a response to a change in internal dynamics or some other significant event in the environment; the second, that it expresses a mode of adaptation, more like a symptom or character trait that over time becomes synchronous with the personality.

Below I list clinical examples and dilemmas that highlight the issue of environmental impact versus a mysterious modification of the dynamics of the personality.

1. A high school graduate who has always dated and seemed heterosexual goes to college and soon after announces to her parents that she is a lesbian. Is this a case of a permissive environment that allows her to come out, or is it one of handling the separation from mother, or something else?
2. A cross-dresser for more than ten years of his adult life one day decides to stop this behavior and does so with no recurrence for several years. Later in therapy for another symptom, he attributes his cessation of cross-dressing to reading about the symptom in a textbook and gaining insight from that information. What other factors operating in his world led to this remarkable transformation?
3. Two seemingly happily married, heterosexual men in their late forties find themselves drawn repeatedly to homosexual bars and furtive homosexual affairs. One goes into therapy with a straight therapist and decides to declare himself gay; the other visits a gay therapist and after treatment returns to

his wife and previous sexual patterns. Are these midlife crises episodes of depression with no particular significance for the perverse behavior, or is there something more to be explained here? If it is primarily a question of a dynamic conflict, then the therapist's sexual orientation should be irrelevant. Regardless of the anecdotal nature of the examples, a substantial folklore insists that the nature of the therapist is important, and there is also a literature (Isay 1989) that insists that gay therapists should treat gay patients. Other than the rather superficial reason that like-minded therapists will better understand similarly oriented patients, there does seem to be a need for a better explanation, and, interestingly enough, these clinical anecdotes are contrary to expectations, although true.

It may seem obvious, but it bears repeating that psychodynamics do not exist in isolation within the patient's psyche; the environment sanctions certain behavior and inhibits others, relieves and diminishes some, and on occasion eradicates others. Sexual behavior in a particular cultural setting may be seen as allowed or encouraged, prohibited or denied, and even, when a perversion, treated and cured.

My second point on the vertical split involves the concept of belief and disbelief, reality and fantasy, and recognition of a percept while denying its meaning or significance. The tenets behind the concept concern a developmental line of reality as well as an agreed-upon consideration of what constitutes reality. The implicit, accepted assumption is that a given culture shares a common set of beliefs. As mentioned earlier, the disavowal of the missing penis is a prototype for all types of splitting. Another assumed idea is that children do indeed have a shared cognitive or epistemological timetable of development. Nevertheless, we know that beliefs vary from family to family as well as from society to society and, except for a few unarguable sets of beliefs, that there is an enormous range of convictions about truth and falsehood. A child is raised with direction and knowledge about the world and its constituents that may differ from one parent to another as well as from parents to representatives outside the family. No one grows up with a coherent set of truths about the nature of things or people in the world. In a sense we are all split about what to make of the external world. The same holds with regard to our selves. We have contradictory viewpoints about ourselves at times, about others at times, and about the things of the world. The lack of a neat correspondence between persons' ideas about the external world and the real condition of that world makes some disavowal necessary in all of us. This universal psychic mechanism can be made more particular in terms of seeing whether it is more or less severe in different states of pathology. This may be the point of departure for the work Glover indicated was needed. The denial of reality and the concomitant split might seem different, perhaps more severe, in a transsexual, for instance, than in a homosexual; this may be a clue to what factors affect the psyche of the developing child in promoting one form of vertical split rather than another. A better and more rational line of development of the reality sense is called for: one that includes the emerging cognitive capacities of the child, the affective components that give meaning to the reality that is sensed, and the multiple visions of reality the child must sift through and come to terms with. We would have to abandon the idea of a singular and agreed-upon real world as an ultimate aim for recognition. Even the gender of the child would be a topic for disagreement since most people feel bisexual at some time or other.

It does seem capricious to include nonsexual activities as perversions. Obsessions such as hair pulling, rituals, and any overt, nonstandard behavior should be excluded from the definition of perversions, which are sexual. Certain forms of sexual activity, such as homosexuality, demand at least two categories: those that are chronic, habitual, and seemingly egosyntonic versus those that are sporadic, furtive, and lead to depression and anxiety. That the second may move to the first may certainly be true in permissive environments, but a group of dystonic perversions remains. These seem more sensitive to environmental influences and may thereby warrant the appellation of sexualization of an effort that goes beyond sexual activity for its own sake: an idea that shall expand upon. That idea will need to be correlated with Freud's concept of the "undoing" of achievements in the course of development. Thus begins a new consideration of perversion as a sexualization rather than an expression of sexuality. I reserve the latter term for varieties of sexual behavior that are not responsive to the narcissistic insults most literature ascribes to perversions. Homosexual individuals are the best examples of persons able to pursue their sexual lives in the service of a well-structured psyche, just as heterosexuals do. Yet we still hope to discover whether such persons use and conform to the other two features of perversion—the particular dynamics and the disavowed feature. It may well be that such a consideration of sexualization will allow the characterization of any sexual activity, including heterosexuality, as perverse, while allowing the delineation of some other sexuality, including nonheterosexual orientations, as falling outside that category. The entire concept of perverse behavior may be turned on its head. Thus the union of the three elements for perversion will surely constrain the looseness of usage that has invaded the field. If we insist on a threefold combination for a new definition, then we should examine and expand the following conclusions:

1. Many dynamic explanations are possible in the study of perverse sexual behavior. They range from preoedipal to oedipal scenarios as well as those that focus on narcissistic issues. No doubt one's allegiance to a theory will be a major determinant of a given dynamic explanation, and no doubt certain formulations will more often fall into one constellation of disorders than another. The familiar story of an absent or passive father and a dominant, phallic mother noted in the histories of some homosexuals is a case in point. But these dynamic forces are

never sufficient explanations, as necessary as they may be. Too many individuals with the same dynamics share only the story and not the pathology. Too many forms of sexual perversion are unable to offer the kind of story we might expect. Thus our psychodynamic formulations function only as partial answers. They allow treatment to be only partially successful; the flaw lies in considering their interpretation and their working through as effective. Beyond right or wrong, they are incomplete answers that may serve to guide a therapist while unwittingly limiting his or her vision.

2. A split in the psyche is a condition of all people suffering from perverse disorders. Freud's fundamental thesis regarding the splitting of the ego in cases of fetishism extends to all perversions and is manifest in the clinical situation in contradictory views of reality with varying or alternating levels of dominance. This duality is termed a vertical split by Kohut and Chasseguet-Smirgel, and more particularly a divided self by Kohut. It may be well for now to call the split a disavowal, a term that covers a range from complete nonregistration to recognition without the significance of emotional impact—the latter a definition preferred by Basch as being most faithful to Freud. Regardless of the name, the condition is not peculiar to perversions, although it is, once again, a necessary but not sufficient aspect of perversions. There may, however, be a hope for a more accurate classification in organizing these disorders on the basis of the nature or severity of the disavowal. This was first suggested by Glover and carries on the attempt by Sander Ferenczi to arrange a developmental line for the sense of reality. Thus far, there is no agreed-upon system of development, because of the common fallacy that some end point of maturity exists and that a false notion may inhibit our better ordering of such a healthy development. It also seems to be accepted that splitting runs across all diagnostic categories and is not correlated with one disorder or another. Although we often invoke a quantitative connection, such as

insisting on severe splitting in borderline disorders, we have thus far been unable to particularize the relation.

3. There is no perversion without sexuality, and for that behavior, sexualization is the keyword. This element, joined with the other two, circumscribes those disorders that are to be separated from all forms of sexual behavior that have no pathology with this characteristic. The form belonging to psychopathology is sexualization, and this must somehow fit with elements of psychodynamics and disavowal, and as a unity, deliver a definition that goes beyond any single portion of the whole. Once this is delineated it will, in turn, be seen as distinct and separate from those sexual behaviors, regardless of their dynamics, that do not reflect pathology. Perverse behavior is defined as such if, and only if, all three of these constituents prevail; of necessity, it becomes a specific psychological entity.

To develop the definition further, each component must be fleshed out. The forms of sexual behavior that do not participate in the tripartite combination require an explanation of their own. I begin by clarifying the nature of sexualization: what it is, when it happens, and how it is related to the world in both its onset and purpose.

2
Sexualization and Desexualization

It is a paradox that psychoanalysis, which has so often been considered as founded on the recognition of sexuality, should itself struggle to make clear the concept of sexualization that at its simplest equates it with misplaced sexuality. Freud said that an organ that is sexualized behaves like a cook who is having a love affair with the master of the house and no longer wants to work in the kitchen: the sexuality has taken over. This is the sexualization of a nonsexual activity (Fenichel 1945), the intrusion of the sexual drive into an arena where it does not belong. Implicit in this characterization of sexualization is the notion that the sexual impulse, ever active in seeking expression, tries to capture some other activity or function in order to assert itself. Once sexualized, that otherwise nonsexual activity is unable to pursue its ordinary path, as though an extra burden had been added to the simplest of tasks. What I propose in this chapter is that sexualization is essentially a lack of available structure, while its disappearance, called desexualization, is evidence of the appearance or reappearance of psychological structure.

The neat Freudian version of sexualization has become more complicated over the years. This complexity arises from two sources. The first is Heinz Hartmann's (1964) consideration of the instinctualization of ego functions, which is seen as indicative of a regressive move of the ego, or a breakdown of the ego's intactness. Hartmann's concepts of instinctualization and its corollary, neutralization, were elaborations of Freud's ideas, but they necessarily expanded the idea of sexualization so that a mere "disturbance of function" could be a sign of sexualization. And so sexualization may exist without sex. The second source of confusion arose from the use of the term *sexualization* as a defense. Here the word was linked more clearly to the activity of or fantasies about sexuality, either normal or pathological, as employed for defensive purposes. Something more than regression is needed to complete the picture, since the ego employs and deploys sexual activity for defensive purposes, from handling anxiety to warding off fantasies of homosexuality (Blum 1973). So just as we allow for sexualization with no manifestation of sex, we have multiple forms of sexual activity without any true sexual meaning. Though the latter is often termed pseudosexuality, it serves to emphasize how far we have traveled from Freud's original formulation. Surely, there is little hope of understanding the clinical management of sexualization without a better comprehension of its meaning.

The classical or orthodox objective of clinical management of sexualization is its dissolution or transformation through the alchemy of sublimation (Alpert 1949). The movement into the preconscious of a sexually charged fantasy that would ordinarily be repressed calls for defensive maneuvers or a redirection of sexual material into acceptable nonsexual areas. Thus the sadist becomes a surgeon. Hartmann modified this concept of sublimation by introducing the concept of neutralization or deinstinctualization: a stripping of the fantasy of its sexual or aggressive change, which is an energic transformation. Kohut then further elaborated the theory of neutralization in his model of progressive neutralization (Kohut and Seitz 1963), in which these archaic fantasies are slowly moved into the manageable and predictably nonsexual areas of the psyche. How all this is accomplished in psychoanalytic treatment is considered part and parcel of all therapeutic intervention, no different from the management of any other repressed psychic material. Yet true sexualization is different. It is sometimes pleasurable, often habitual, and rarely capable of a shift in category. Although the scientist may be a sublimated voyeur, it is a rare voyeur who is transformed into a scientist through psychoanalysis.

In a shift of emphasis, I offer an elaboration of the later Kohut position: Structuralization as the crucial component to the clinical management of sexualization leads not to sublimation but rather to desexualization, the cessation of a reliance on sexualization. This suggestion rests on several premises. The first is that the occurrence of sexualization is a manifestation of a structural deficiency that may or may not be lifelong, but because of special developmental circumstances, is handled in individual cases by sexual fantasies or behavior. Such action serves defensive purposes in forestalling further regression (Kohut 1971), pleasure in mastery, and sexual pleasure in its own right. The structural deficiency, now termed a defect, however, is often temporarily filled by other persons, and so sexualization is forestalled until this temporary solution is lost, that is, the filling in becomes unavailable.

The second premise is that psychoanalytic treatment is effective in patients who sexualize when and if the analyst can fill the structural deficit in the patient's psychological makeup and, over time, restore the damaged psychic structure. This position is to be clearly distinguished from those of the analyst as the target of the patient's drives, participant in an intersubjective or interpersonal field of the patient, superego component controlling the patient's drives, and educator who trains the apractic patient to develop psychological competences lacking before the analytic encounter. The filling in of psychological structure is indeed an accomplishment of psychoanalytic treatment, but the process of structuralization follows the course of normal development; that is, it is based on phase-specific, nontraumatic opportunities to take over functions rather than on an educational exercise imposed from outside. Structure in this definition is enduring function, and structuralization is the process by which the developing psyche assumes the functions offered by caretakers (Goldberg 1988, 130).

The presence of sexualization in a predominant form in certain patients must be distinguished from its almost universal occurrence in the general population and from the theoretical but essentially nonsexual form proposed by Hartmann. Moving away from the energic concepts allows us to concentrate on a pure form of sexualization reflective of specific structural defects. It also allows us to see that sporadic or occasional sexualization can be more clearly distinguished from the usual or normal forms of sexual activity. In fact, the view (Coen 1981) that sexualization is an aspect of all sexual activity, offered to explain the defensive nature of sexual behavior and fantasy, may obscure more than it clarifies. We need a delineation of sexualization that clearly distinguishes it from otherwise normal sexual activity. Such a delineation would explain, for example, forms of homosexual activity that are considered pathological while others are not. Distinguishing manifestations of sexual fantasy or behavior—that is, the pathological from the normal—can rarely be made either casually or descriptively. One needs the perspective of a psychoanalyst, especially one who can employ a theory of structure and structuralization. Basic concepts from self psychology are that the self is the structure to be considered and evaluated, and the selfobject is a constituent of that structure. The analyst as selfobject fills in a defect of the self. He or she is not a co-participant in a mutual structure inasmuch as the structural needs of the patient fix the unfolding program of analysis. Outbreaks of sexualization occur in and around that function and position of the analyst, a position that serves to compensate for a deficiency in the patient and allows for self experiences that may otherwise have been unavailable to the individual, ultimately allowing the defect to be healed.

Literature Review

There is little to add to the excellent review of the subject of sexualization by Stanley Coen, who, after summarizing the literature, endorsed a solution that would restrict the concept to sexual behavior and fantasy with the goals and functions of defense. The relevant literature covers a discussion of the erotized transference (Blum 1973), the concept of the selfobject, and the sexualization of that structure (Kohut 1971), as well as the issue of the reparative effects of sexualization for the narcissistically vulnerable individual (Stolorow 1975).

The lack of consensus about which sexual behaviors are normal and which are pathological is reviewed by Charles Socarides (1992) in his discussion of homosexuality. He considers the homosexual to be severely handicapped (p. 317) and in a sense as necessarily manifesting a psychological disorder. Socarides bemoans the fact that homosexuality has become free of diagnostic labeling, owing, he says, to political pressures. It remains to be seen whether homosexuality and heterosexuality share in what is essentially a division of purpose; that is, whether an act of sexuality can sometimes be considered sexualization and at other times normal sexuality. This is in keeping with the principle of not reducing perversion to the manifestation of behavior.

Stoller (1990) extended the political implications of sexual activity to the moral dimension by insisting that psychoanalytic ideas be included in evaluations of sexuality. He did not note the implicit morality in the decisions of psychoanalysis about normality and normal development. Sexual behavior seems unable to escape the label of either illness or correctness.

Kernberg (1991) joins Coen in including some perverse activity within the bounds of normal sexual functioning. Kernberg feels that sadomasochism, for example, is an essential part of sexual excitement. He constructs a continuum from normal to psychopathic perversions, which depends on the nature of ego and superego organization. An integrated tripartite structure would yield normal sexuality with predominantly libidinal components; an intermediate realm would reflect borderline and narcissistic personality structures; an extreme structure would conform to the syndromes of malignant narcissism, antisocial personality structures, and psychosis. Kernberg draws heavily on the work of Chasseguet-Smirgel (1986), who has developed some thoughts about the archaic aspects of the Oedipus complex. As we have seen, for Chasseguet-Smirgel all perversions develop against an anal sadomasochistic backdrop, and their aim is to destroy reality. She also considers homosexuality to include a range of disorders from those close to neurosis to those bordering on psychosis. It is not clear whether she would consider some homosexuality as normal or would incorporate an aspect of perversion into normal sexuality, as Kernberg does. The continuum may go just so far.

Clinical Considerations

Perversions or sexualizations span rare and sporadic episodes of behavior, which may or may not be accompanied by feelings of pleasure, to long-lasting, habitual forms of fantasy and action with an equally variable incidence of pleasure. To attribute a particular set of psychodynamics to the operation of sexualization and perversion, as indicated above, would be only a partial explanation at best. To further complicate the problem, the coexistence of seemingly normal heterosexual behavior alongside the most intricate and bizarre forms of sexual activity would counter the possibility of a "schema . . . [that] does apply to all forms of perversion" (Chasseguet-Smirgel 1991, 414). Nor could one possibly explain the behavior of a prominent professional man, happily married and capable of full and completely pleasurable sexual intercourse, who has to dress in women's clothing, put on rouge and lipstick, and masturbate in front of a mirror solely on the basis of his level of personality organization (Kernberg 1991, 334), unless that organization manifests a fluidity that strains our usual diagnostic categories. A purely psychodynamic explanation of perverse sexuality and sexualization is inadequate since there exists for the most part a significant temporal dimension to the appearance of either perverse sexuality or sexualization. The variability of sexualization remains to be explained. It is clear that the appearance of this behavior is tightly linked first to the environment and then to very definite moments in the transference established in the treatment of these cases.

The following case is that of a patient who would probably be regarded by any diagnostician as employing sexualization. The case does not exemplify a particular technique, and it would be handled and conceptualized differently by different therapists under differing theoretical outlooks. What I intend is to alter the reader's perspective on how to evaluate sexualization and thus realign our diagnostic evaluation of all types of sexual disorders. It is presented as a single case example (Edelson 1986), but clinical experience allows for a generalization beyond this instance. The positive findings of many analyses of such cases follow the proposed theory and explain the outcomes better or at least differently. Thus, I offer a new explanation for a not uncommon event.

Case Illustration

Robert, a twenty-seven-year-old lawyer, came for a psychiatric consultation after visits to two mental health professionals for an opinion about his recent decision to come out of the closet as a homosexual. He was unusually unsettled about this decision inasmuch as he had never had a homosexual experience. His entire sexual history consisted of masturbation and one or two furtive and unsuccessful attempts at intercourse with a woman acquaintance. His other consultants encouraged his entrance into the homosexual world and advised that he be counselled in doing so. He considered his more recent consultation to be totally different because the consultant asked about the nature and content of his masturbatory fantasies. He said that they consisted exclusively of sexual activity with older men, usually fellatio. Robert spent much time during an average day searching for this kind of man and immediately told me he knew he must have a "father fixation." His parents had divorced when he was ten years old, and he was quick to say that the divorce had not affected him at all because he had no use for his father either before or after the divorce, a sentiment he still held. His school performance had deteriorated after the divorce, but he attributed this to the need to change schools. He mainly wanted my opinion about his decision to declare himself a homosexual, quit his job, and move to San Francisco.

I told him that I could not begin to understand his sexual uncertainty, but I did feel that his problems had little to do with sex, either homosexual or heterosexual. Intrigued by this response, he made several more visits and then decided to undergo analysis. The overwhelming note of every visit, however, as well as the dominant theme of the beginning stage of the analysis, was the question of whether he was truly homosexual. Although his query was accompanied by a deep shame about that possibility, he held a fatalistic view that as long as he remained interested in middle-aged men his fate seemed certain. My position was primarily one of uncertainty and curiosity; his story was so much the account of a troubled and unhappy person with few close relationships that his sexual preoccupation was secondary.

In the beginning, Robert insisted that he knew for certain just what he was, as if there were an inner fixed reading that confirmed his homosexuality. His intense focus on having a clear decision about his sexuality made me suspect that this preoccupation was a blanket that had been thrown over his entire life, obscuring what was much more essential about him. He carried his focused sexual thinking to all areas of his life, wondering what co-workers, friends, and casual acquaintances thought about him sexually. Did he look effeminate? Did they suspect? Did they secretly make fun of him? He decided to begin analysis ostensibly to learn the truth, but also with a wish for relief from these painful preoccupations.

Robert began analysis with a rare eagerness and enthusiasm, accompanied as time passed by a beginning relationship with a woman colleague to whom he confided most of what he told to me in almost a co-conspiratorial vein. Not long after this beginning, he became sexually intimate with this woman. He had no difficulty in sexual performance and seemed to find intercourse pleasurable and fulfilling. Initially I considered this action to be an example of the patient's defense against the transference. His dreams seemed to confirm that his new-found paramour was being used as a confessor and analyst and that his sexual activity was in the service of avoiding his relationship to me. The interesting point about this rather common form of early resistance was that it was the patient's very first sexual experience; it was also intriguing in view of his concern over his homosexual orientation.

Shortly after the onset of his analysis, Robert began to discuss his homosexual fantasies in detail. Concomitant with this, he found himself having sexual fantasies about another analyst. The fantasies consisted of having anal intercourse with the analyst, penetrating him from the rear. This sexualized displacement of the transference took place when the patient had to make a presentation to customers and senior colleagues. It was initially interpreted as a transposition to the sexual arena of his anxious feelings. The fantasy went on to include the analyst explaining the mechanisms of sex to the patient, followed by a fantasy of the patient watching an actor on television having intercourse with a woman while the patient concentrated on the actor's penis penetrating the woman's vagina. The patient's associations were to an upcoming work assignment that involved asking an older associate for guidance and instruction. The patient was highly anxious about doing it without help, and the older man was an expert at the task. I interpreted the fantasy as a sexualization of the anxiety, along with a beginning dependence on getting help from his analyst. His further association dealt with yet another masturbatory fantasy: performing fellatio on this television actor while carefully studying his face and breathing. Robert's concentration was on what the man was doing and experiencing. This fantasy was also interpreted as referring to Robert's curiosity about me. The patient said, "There's this big emptiness in me, and it's right in the middle of my chest. There is this longing for a man, but it's not sexual with you as it is with other men. If it were sexual with you, it would be horrible and that would end the analysis."

As the analysis proceeded, material came out representing events that might ordinarily have given rise to a series of emotions seemingly lost in the scenarios of sex. The transition to a more open experience of these affect states followed an hour of alternating fantasies of heterosexual and homosexual activity. Robert told of feeling that he was a "geek," that he looked foolish, hated his body, worried about his skin and hair, and constantly suspected that people were making fun of him. The display of shameful feelings made me feel that he was now more able to commit himself to me, and shortly thereafter the sexualization disappeared. Although this waxing and waning of sexual preoccupation may be characteristic of many such cases, the disappearance in this case was dramatic, as the patient had insisted that his mind had rarely, if ever, been free of such thoughts for long.

As If by Magic

The cessation of sexualization during the course of an analysis is not unusual, and I deal with it in detail in the chapter on treatment. It may, however, be either a dramatic or a gradual event and should, of course, always be differentiated from whatever normal sexual activity is proceeding in the life of the patient. When a lifting of sexualization takes place, it is occasion for consideration and study in the developing transference. Certainly, in some patients much analytic work must be done to allow the transference to be realized, but sometimes, as Kohut (1971) said, it merely "clicks into place." Once realized, we begin to see the aforementioned filling in of the structural defect.

In this patient, one particular visit stood out as a turning point. It began with his commenting on how much he liked to come in and just talk. He then reported a dream about playing with two dachshunds, one of which seemed to hold on to him. A second dream was about his sitting between his father and his brother-in-law, when, after a moment, his father began to put his hands on the patient in a sexual way. The patient did not know how to respond. He next remarked that he was feeling threatened in opening up to me. He recalled the previous visit, when he brought up his irritation at being charged for missed hours. He was startled that I had agreed to discuss the matter instead of merely insisting that the rule was agreed upon. He thereupon saw the connection to the dream and asked himself why he turned anxiety into sexual things. There then followed a portrait of the father as an enigma, someone who never revealed anything. The two dogs and the two men represented the father who never talked and a heretofore-unmentioned uncle who always talked to Robert, to his delight.

After this visit, the patient noted that he no longer had to masturbate and no longer had sexual fantasies, especially about the other analyst, whom he felt was really me. As the visits progressed he connected more to me, to missing me when I was gone, to wanting to be my favorite, to wanting a gift from me, and so forth. The father who was both missing and a mystery began to live and be discovered in analysis.

An example of the reappearance of sexualization, which is a regular and expectable feature of treatments like this, occurred at a point that some might consider a disruption or empathic break. The patient anticipated a schedule conflict and called to alert me and to inquire about rescheduling the appointment, which I was unable to do. He did, however, keep the appointment, and he reported a dream of a baby being held by its hair and an earlier incident of masturbation. The latter was accompanied by a fantasy of his undressing the male actor he had fantasized about before and examining him, as though he, the patient, were a doctor. He was primarily intent on studying the man's face and immediately connected this fact to his curiosity about me and what I thought of him and his usual sexual litany. It went further this time, however, to his feeling that the baby of the dream was himself being mistreated by me in my ungracious reception of his request. Yet he was now, in the fantasy, the doctor in charge. The next step was his conviction of himself as bad or disgusting because of his sexual proclivities and also because he was demanding and needy—a bother. In short order we together saw him as wanting to intrude upon his preoccupied father, who responded with the unspoken but unmistakable message, "Don't bother me."

The following is an example of the rage and hostility associated with sexuality. The actual sequence is that a patient misses several appointments and becomes fascinated by a man in a locker room. He cannot keep from staring, especially at the man's penis, which is strikingly large. He continues to think about the man and at one point tries to imagine the man having intercourse with a woman but feels that this was an effort to escape his conviction that he is homosexual. He masturbated with a series of images of looking at the man and his penis and also performing fellatio. He was mortified and embarrassed to report this in analysis. In fact, he recalled his intense rage at his father as responsible for his (the patient's) "screwed up" mental health. He reports a dream in which he is escaping from the Viet Cong with several others. The scene is the apartment the family lived in after his parents' divorce. The escapees run to a vehicle, where the patient is forced to sit extremely close to the driver. He wakes with the conviction that the driver is his analyst and that he is destined to stay in analysis as long as he is so plagued by disturbing sexual thoughts. The Viet Cong of the dream represent his rage at his father, a rage that he seems unable to overcome, much as he felt when a child. Here we see evidence of the anger and hostility that accompany perversion in its sequence of occurrence but that are quintessentially a reaction to a passive fate.

Discussion

The concept of structural deficiency is sort of a grab bag of ideas that is often used to explain that patients are unable to feel, do, or think certain things because of a lack in their psyche. That missing feature is not, however, signaled merely by a vacancy, but by forms of exposure that display its presence. Kohut followed his explication of selfobjects by suggesting that some perverse activity was a sexualization of a selfobject to forestall regression (that is, an active move to overcome the passive experience of losing the selfobject). A beginning conceptualization to indicate the function the selfobject serves is offered in *Models of the Mind*. It came in the form of positing the object as one of unification and its gradual loss as optimal disillusion. An additional and important elaboration was supplied by Basch (1988) in his discussion of affect attunement, which described the need to have a shared affective experience to allow for an interaction that would form a healthy self, which in turn acknowledges the need for the participation of other persons in one's life. Analysts were soon able to chart a psyche that handled a developmental defect in a certain way, compensated for it in a sometimes effective manner, struggled in treatment to participate in the repair of that developmental mishap, and ultimately reorganized itself in a changed structure.

A map of a patient's psyche is a system that extends to the selfobjects that constitute the patient's self. For some individuals the continued presence of these constituent selfobjects allows for a psychic equilibrium that seems unshakable. Yet the absence of one or more of them may lead to a beginning disintegration. In the sexual sphere we may see this as the sudden outbreak of homosexual or other perverse behavior in the life of an otherwise heterosexual man or woman, commonly during a midlife crisis. For many other patients there is never a stable or semi-stable set of selfobjects in their world, so sexualization may dominate their lives and soon become so chronic that long periods of analytic treatment are needed to allow a semblance of a workable transference. Perhaps the majority of patients have periods of stability along with instability. We can therefore observe and explain the coexistence of sexualization and normal sexual activity. The proposed thesis is: Normal sexual activity requires a stable and cohesive self and can be achieved only in the context of that structure. Sexuality is thus the act of a strong and stable self, resulting from the vigor of a consolidated self. Sexualization temporarily shores up the self. It occurs when one or another of the deployed selfobjects is endangered.

I now return to an examination of disturbed sexuality in light of a disturbance of structuralization. First, the coexistence of perverse and normal sexuality can be explained as being a result of fluctuations in the presence and availability of sustaining selfobjects. The development from archaic to mature selfobjects is not a movement from outside to inside but rather is a change in the self's capacity to use selfobjects flexibly and adaptively (Goldberg 1990). Thus, persons are not totally with or without selfobjects but have a variable and changeable repertoire of selfobjects. Treatment increases one's capacity to use and to hold them.

A result of this perspective is a reconsideration of homosexuality. It may truly be either normal or perverse. One form may be a manifestation of a choice of a sexual object that is satisfying and fulfilling regardless of the particular set of psychodynamics. As such, it is not changeable by psychoanalytic intervention. As an example, I outline the particulars of a type of homosexual behavior as a compensatory structure that can never be analyzed to yield an altered sexual preference but can nonetheless benefit from analysis. Other forms of homosexual *behavior* indicate a sexualization to gain and maintain a selfobject link. These more troubled individuals can be helped by analytic treatment, but the resulting, more stable self may still yield a homosexual choice. The natural extension of this viewpoint is the position that any sexual behavior, including heterosexuality, is a possible expression of a vulnerable self given to sexualization. There are thus two problems in assessing the sexual behavior of an individual, as presented in the above case, whose presenting bisexuality gave no certain clues to the resultant sexuality. Only when we determine that the sexual behavior serves primarily and exclusively to save the person from self fragmentation can we see it as sexualization. To this, society's allowance or repugnance of the behavior must be added in assessing its pathology.

It is not the case that certain forms of sexual activity, such as sadomasochism, are necessary precursors or companions of sexual activity that is considered to be the norm. Rather, it is more likely that all sexual activity is an admixture of sexualization and sexuality, with the former shoring up the self in order to participate more fully in the latter. My experience in the analytic treatment of some perversions suggests another category of patients, those who after the resolution of their sexualized fantasies and behavior, show relatively little interest in sexual activity. This seems to be a more striking indicator of the pseudosexual quality of the behavior. Although it may be viewed as sublimation, it is equally likely that a reconstituted self has several options to pursue, and the usual anxieties associated with sexual behavior preclude those pursuits.

Thus we must be ever more alert to the dual problem of politicalization and moralization (see chapter 6). Psychoanalysis is no different from others in this regard, since it includes standards for the determination of normal behavior, and full sexual fulfill-

ment is certainly one of those standards. It requires a radical
shift from our usual criteria of good health to consider someone
to be normal whose efforts at such fulfillment in the sexual realm
are rare or nonexistent. Just as we may relieve a person of frantic
sexualizations of survival, we should be equally eager to see to it
that some people do without it altogether.

Sexualization is demonstrated in individuals who employ it
to avoid painful affects (Blos 1991), to shore up a vulnerable self,
to ward off a regressive movement following the loss of a sustaining relationship, and for other defensive purposes (Coen 1981).
It is seen in psychoanalysis as a resistance to the development
of the transference, as an indicator of a beginning but not
well-established transference, and as a sign of a disruption in
transference. It regularly diminishes and disappears in psychoanalytic treatment as the transference is stabilized, and it often
becomes a barometer of the vicissitudes of the transference. If
the transference is in a state of equilibrium, if a patient feels
understood, sexualization is unnecessary. During states of empathic disruption and the physical or emotional absence of the
analyst, sexualization is once again called upon.

Desexualization bespeaks a structural modification that demonstrates the tolerance of otherwise disavowed or unex-
perienced affects, a more solid and cohesive self, a progressive
developmental step, and an entrance into possibly new emotional experiences. It is seen in psychoanalysis during moments
of transference stability, in which both new information and
reactivated points in the past become the currency of analytic
work. Its loss in analysis is a sign of a movement of either the
patient or the analyst that destroys the connection. Its reestablishment often marks progression in the analysis.

Rather than sublimation, which is a redirection of a libidinal
drive, or neutralization, which is a de-instinctualization of a
drive, the concept of structuralization is offered as explanatory
of desexualization, defined as the entrance of a stable selfobject

into the psychological field of the patient. This link demonstrates a stable transference, and psychoanalytic work aims to increase the stability and competence of the self, composed as it is of its selfobjects.

Differentiating sexualization from sexuality might offer an opportunity to distinguish forms of sexual behavior that are manifestly similar but psychologically distinct. We might then be able to realign our diagnostic considerations as to the feasibility and advisability of altering or modifying such sexual behavior.

Next I examine in more detail the nature of the structure that self psychologists refer to as defective or weakened and split. It is of the utmost importance to recognize how psychoanalysis uses the idea of structure and to realize just what is meant by structuralization.

3

The Study of the Self as
Psychic Structure

It is important to place the idea of the structure of psycho-analysis in context. Although it is possible to talk about it as split or weak or defective, these terms are evocative rather than de-scriptive. It is better to delineate what a psychological structure is and how it is formed, weakened, strengthened, and depleted.

The man who is considered the founder of French semantics and a forerunner of the philosophy of structuralism, Ferdinand de Saussure (1916), offered an illustration of the concept of structure. The 8:05 train from Paris to Geneva arrives in Geneva regularly at approximately 8:05 and is thus distinguished from the 7:05 and the 10:05. It is composed of an engine and a number of cars, but these are not necessarily the same from one day to the next: one day new cars are used and the next day old ones. Neither the composition nor the elements of the train need be constant in order for it to be the 8:05 train. Its position in the general pattern of train arrivals and departures is the single issue in considering it the 8:05. *Structuralism*, similarly, directs our attention to the forms and patterns by which the composite ele-ments relate to one another, at the same time lessening our atten-tion to the particular composition of those elements. To be sure, we often identify a particular element as essentially embodying the structure: a favorite seat on a favorite train might lead one to feel that she is riding the "old 8:05" as it wends its way to a different destination at a different time. It may seem folly to try to distinguish form from content or pattern from composition, since they remain inextricable. However, much work in fields allied to psychoanalysis—for example, linguistics, and especially the work of Noam Chomsky—has prospered under just such a distinction. For language, it may simply be a matter of separating syntax or formal structure from semantics, but for psychoanalysis the task is different.

For psychoanalysis, a similar project may offer a fruitful road of inquiry. The procedure for a psychoanalytic division of labor between pattern and elements would be to decide on a proper object of study—for example, the ego—for its pattern or organization and then to determine whether the pattern and its stability would override issues of composition, which would then become secondary (the 8:05 may use cars with seats of red plastic as well as yellow leather). The implications of this investigation may or may not be far ranging, but certainly over time they would modify our concepts of health and disease so that we could classify disorders as primary and secondary. Those having to do with basic organization would be the primary determinants of psychopathology, whereas secondary elements would lend only color and shape to the basic program.

There exist many mental phenomena that exhibit structure, whether defined as innate constraints, the capacity to act, or enduring function. Visual perception, for example, is a mental process limited by the quality of light rays that stimulate it. It is evoked in a learned manner that can be investigated, as, for example, by raising kittens in the dark or by ablating neuronal pathways. It has adapted in special ways in various cultures so that certain things are perceived in particular, learned ways—such as snow by the Innuit. All mental processes may naturally become involved in a psychoanalytic investigation, but not all will be relevant to the analytic situation and a readiness for change with analytic intervention, thus narrowing the task.

If, following Kohut (1971), we select the self rather than the ego as the basic form or organization we will study, then principles as well as questions present themselves. The self is a stable configuration at certain periods of life and will undergo modification according to rules and regulations during growth and development. Any other organization we would choose to study, whether inside or outside human psychology or biology, likewise preserves fixed aspects that allow it to be considered stable over time, even though it may undergo extensive modifications and even dramatic recastings. The fixed form of the self is thus a phenomenon of varied manifestations throughout a person's life. Any particular method of studying this form, such as psychoanalysis, will reveal crucial or dominant types of the configuration that allow us to consider the form in its plural sense— that is, different selves at different times. A transformation of a fixed and relatively stable form means not only that the configuration appears different—that is, it operates differently from the usual—but also that a different set of rules governs the operation of the system. Thus, when we see a particular person or self-system engaged in a creative pursuit, we can say that the self is in a transformed state and is functioning according to a different program or set of plans. To be sure, such a conclusion is valid only according to the method of inquiry being employed and the kind of data one is able to gather. It follows that the psychoanalytic observation of creative persons may or may not reveal that which is crucial to the particular operations of a creative self. We are studying a complex network that shows different forms, does different things at different times, and even changes itself over time.

When we say that a form operates under specific rules, these range from the constraints imposed by the physical limits of the system (for example, the retina is not responsive to certain wavelengths of light) to the limits imposed by the particular environment (certain behaviors are more acceptable in some places than in others, and certain behaviors are strictly forbidden). Unfortunately, psychoanalysis does not always have a neat set of rules for observing the proper or healthy operations of the phenomena we study. We are likewise uncertain about the rules we follow in our therapeutic encounters. Either explicitly or implicitly, however, we presume a normative program in developmental lines and in the process of analytic treatment. Such rules are evidence of the proper functioning of the observed system, and in a somewhat circular fashion we say that our evaluation of structure is based on unchanging or slowly changing function.

The elements of a structure call for an important point of differentiation. If an organization is operating smoothly under predetermined rules and procedures, then the particular aspects of one or another part of the pattern are of secondary importance, becoming part of the background. Just as the 8:05 is considered to be doing its job if it arrives, departs, and delivers its passengers on schedule, so a self functions well if it follows its own set of plans. The makeup of the train, although of interest, is not of primary relevance, nor is the makeup of the ego or self-organization. According to Kohut (1971), mirroring, for example, would be a function that can sometimes be carried out by various selfobjects without attention to their individual personalities. If we grant this assumption, we might go so far as to say that the particular meanings attributed to a given form of ideation or behavior by a person are *delivered* by the self-system, but perhaps they are also essentially of secondary significance. I offer the idea that a specific meaning is subsumed under the momentary functioning of the self. *The structure delivers the meaning.* It is the framework within which meaning and its associated term, *understanding*, are able to operate and be articulated. Just as rules and regulations demand a more elaborate description, so too does this complex notion of meaning. For now, we note that our attention to particular moments of meaning may detract from our comprehension of the underlying framework or matrix within which it lies and can be expressed.

A true structural psychology that makes structural considerations the basis of our study of individuals can be outlined. One aspect of behavior may mean something that can be decoded, much as Freud and his successors in psychoanalysis have done with symptoms, parapraxes, and jokes. Hence, there is a story told within each such unpacking of mental complexes. It is also the case that the delivery of the symptom or joke reflects an underlying structure that is revealed with the phenomenon being scrutinized. Some stories are decipherable only when this structure is intact, and whether or not the story is demonstrated in one manner or another is of secondary importance. There is no doubt that much of modern psychoanalysis has assumed a structural integrity as a given and thereupon has devoted itself wholly to the intriguing task of investigating the varied forms of meaning an intact structure would deliver. Here we see the myriad ways in which the oedipal conflict is lived out. Still, perhaps a case can be made that this is essentially a misplaced emphasis inasmuch as it is the system that merits our attention. To pursue my analogy, the train tracks must be intact. What emerges from the system is understanding (Goldberg 1988), that is, the self delivers a meaning to someone who then understands it.

A therapist tells of a patient seen years earlier in a long analysis. He describes her retrospectively, using the idiolect of modern psychoanalysis while emphasizing that his ideas at the time were not those of today. When he first saw the patient she fit the criteria of a borderline personality, and her treatment was consistent with the pattern of work for the category of disorder. After a period she seemed to improve and assumed the appearance and behavior of what we today call a narcissistic personality disorder. We assume that the analyst's experience and knowledge led him to these categories from a correlated appearance of the appropriate transference manifestations. He continued his analysis of the patient, and over time she showed what he described as classical oedipal problems, with the concomitant display of jealousy, rivalry, and intensely competitive issues. The analysis was terminated, apparently successfully, after the supposed resolution of these belatedly revealed conflicts. After termination, the patient continued to correspond with the analyst, and, to his dismay, a reverse regression ensued. She wrote irregularly but often enough for him to see the gradual deterioration of her condition to the point where he was considering her to be once again a typical borderline personality, with episodes of near paranoia, addictive propensities, and a fairly isolated condition. He attributed much of the deterioration to the loss of important real figures in her life, but he remained puzzled about why the treatment did not hold. One might say that the patient demonstrated a structural regression, but it is not clear whether her improvement was equally a structural progression. If we concentrate on what are essentially the secondary phenomena of personality organization, we may see that patients tell essentially different stories at different times in their (and our) lives. But the stories need not correlate or exist in parallel with the condition of the structure. Schizophrenic patients often have vivid oedipal conflicts. This patient may have used her therapist to ensure self-integrity. Yet without becoming the central focus of the interpretive work of her treatment, it soon evaporated under the stress of her life.

The question that naturally arises is, how does one pay attention to issues of pattern or organization that we consider evidence of structural integrity or structural defect? Are our accustomed investigations of meanings an inappropriate avenue to determine levels of psychopathology, and are we indeed listening to the words instead of the music? Perhaps equally important, might our attention to the nuances and particulars of our patients' narratives sometimes be beside the point? Might we be listening to a set of meanings at a different level from those that reveal the state of integrity of the system? I will show that these individual stories are simply not-good-enough guides to our assessment of the patient's self and underlying psychopathology.

To answer the question of how one determines and then attends to the level of communication that reflects a condition of underlying structure rather than address the secondary characteristics of the presentation, we must separate a category of data that is appropriate to the posed problem. That requires, first, clarification of the nature of the connections that make up the organized whole. How do aspects of the self come together? This mechanism reveals itself as any self-selfobject link does. It is in the communicative process that we find how parts of the self system join up, and it is in the process of understanding that we unravel the complex matrix of meaning. People connect to one another by a series of affective exchanges that run the gamut of gestures and verbal exchanges from infancy to adulthood. This intricate web of connections constitutes the structure of self-organization. The messages exchanged between persons travel along a system that must allow for the delivery of particular meanings. The process may sound more mysterious than it is meant to be. It merely separates the conditions for understanding, such as the mutual possession of a common language, from the actual message that is being sent and received. In the psycho-analytic situation, the task is to see the transference as a medium that allows communication between patient and analyst rather than as something primarily about the mother or about the father. Thus the establishment of a workable transference is first to be seen as an avenue of communication, a way to make oneself understood. Only after that pathway is formed can we add the particulars of the message.

Railroads do many things: they deliver goods and people, are a part of the local and national economy, are objects of aesthetic enjoyment for some people and phobic objects for others. These various functions are, however, not actual units of the railroad, like the parts that make up the depot, the barns, and the trains. Rather, they are simultaneously operating functions that evoke different, selective, and quantitatively varied attention. One must take care in choosing whether the units of the self have to do with varied emergent functions or with other constituent elements. What makes up the self has to do with its underlying structure. To say that it consists of units that connect with objects, past and present, unconscious wishes, superego and ego goals, and the necessary ego faculties is one way of encompassing it, to not be confused with the underlying organization and its many operative capacities. So, too, we can say that the self (of whatever composition) does many things simultaneously, and that the same self shows different aspects at different times. Complex wholes certainly do allow one aspect to dominate at one time or another, but these aspects are not units any more than the place of the railroad in the country's overall transportation system is a unit. A puzzle thus presents itself as to where and whether one can effectively distinguish the basic structure from the simpler and more complex phenomena perceived.

We are faced with the problem of exactly what a self is made of when we try to differentiate its basic components—say, arms and legs—from basic representations, such as fathers and workers. In the same way, we may attempt to separate a basic configuration of a system.

It is tempting to see the self as composed of units and to follow its growth as one builds a whole from the units. This may not be possible and may defeat the idea that the self is a whole or a set as it comes into being and so is not made up of smaller parts. There may be a vagueness in our determination of the elements of the self, which as a whole can thus far be defined only as the network of relations (the connections) that makes for understanding. A patient, for instance, tells of making several appointments with friends over a weekend in order to stabilize and regulate himself and prevent the regressive disorganization that occurs when he is left to his own devices. One of his appointments was abruptly canceled by a friend, and subsequently the patient did experience the expected state of disorganization. Although the patient insisted that the missed meeting was merely a nodal point or a precipitant of his feeling out of sorts, the therapist could not let it rest at that since he wondered whether there were not accompanying feelings of hurt and anger at what was essentially a rejection. Was this an example of fragile structure held intact by a schedule with fairly replaceable others, or a case where one needed to examine the particular nature of the relation, beyond basic organization? Here is the dilemma of looking at the structure itself and at the meaning delivered. The railroad can be said to be made up of tracks and trestles or nuts and bolts, but this differs from having a definable unit as a basic structure. We choose such a unit on the basis of its special place in the overall form. For the railroad it may be the Paris-Geneva connection rather than a car or a depot; for the person it is a meaningful relation rather than a body or a body part.

Determining a meaningful overall form of the self should therefore be the fundamental goal of our study. The form will in turn be composed of relations or connections. Though its many manifestations or representations display various messages or meanings, we look beyond these phenomena to the underlying structure. The structure, then, consists of a set of relations, has fixed forms, and delivers many meanings as it is represented. Similarly, a railroad consists of trains and tracks and serves many functions for the community and environment in which it operates. There are three levels: the nuts and bolts, the basic structure or organization, and the multitude of observable activities or representations. As I will show, there is a correlation between the three elements of perversion mentioned earlier: the structural failure, which leads to sexualization, the split, which alters the person's relation to the world, and individual dynamics, which tell how he or she got to that point.

A Closer Look at the Levels

Since any word, concept, or object can be seen to have many meanings, one can never be certain of a single or main assigned meaning. A patient's distress over the cancellation of an appointment may be because of a fantasy about what could have been done in the missing time, a specific reaction to the manner in which the cancellation was handled, or to an irregularity introduced into an accustomed sequence. We may take comfort in the assumption that the "real" meaning will arise during the associations, but this can be false comfort. The patient's associations *do* deliver meanings, but analysts do not always hear them. It is in the first of our three levels, the underlying elements of the structure, that this is often the case.

Evidence of problems on the level of the building blocks of the structure is seen in those cases whose stability depends on the apparently contentless aspects of treatment. Patients who seem to "pull themselves together" or reintegrate when they are hospitalized or put under a strict schedule are said to use the environment as structure, but it is often unclear what the structure is. The improvement of adolescents under various forms of external control or limit setting is explained in a similar manner. Analytic patients who are interested primarily in the rules and regulations of the analytic setting and whose stable transferences seem to dissolve with small changes in setting are also members of this group. Indeed, no one seems totally immune to a potential state of agitation that demands a settling down period (see Gedo and Goldberg 1971 for an extensive discussion of pacification). The major factor in such tension regulation is that it seems relatively free of psychological content (or meaning) and does not yet qualify for inclusion in one or another form of transference. The range of pathology goes from the narcissistically vulnerable person, for whom an average day is a series of horrible rebuffs, injuries, and disruptions, to the well-adjusted person, whose move to a new home or office requires a long period of getting things in their place and getting oneself in proper alignment with everything. Such conditions lend themselves nicely to metaphors of construction—psychological glue, the nuts and bolts of everyday life, the holding environment, and so forth. Using a communication metaphor, we would probably say that all the wiring is in place; in a social service agency, that the support network is intact.

Here may be the entry point for a consideration of sexualization as a reaction to the breakup of the system. These efforts of activity are responses to a threatened disintegration, and the objects of sexual activity are thereby seen as a part or parts of the entire structure. Thus, just as the sexualization demonstrates the onset of a loss of integrity, the desexualization shows us how the structure is once again solidified and made intact. Here the emphasis is on the activity per se as a process aimed at holding things together. That the sexual activity also reveals something of the patient's history and present life goes without saying, but at this level it serves stability only.

The category we seek to delineate by the introduction of the building blocks for stability is, once again, to be separated from the nature of the messages carried by the intact wires. The messages have to do with a consideration of the concept of understanding. The intactness of the structure is a prerequisite for a message being sent and understood. Though everyone can claim a sense of ownership or individuality for those structures that constitute the building blocks of the self, more often than not they are exchangeable, interchangeable, and easily adapted.

The distinction of the second level is that it is a specific form of organization. It is shaped by and composed of the kinds of selfobject transferences that Kohut (1971) described, and thus it serves particular functions, primarily in the regulation and maintenance of self-esteem. The connecting links between self and selfobject that constitute this form—that is, a stable configuration over time—are themselves composed of affective exchanges that fall under the broad rubric of understanding. We relate to or communicate with one another by virtue of empathic exchanges, by which we say that we understand one another. Certainly, much human exchange can and does take place without the ingredient of empathy, and there seems little doubt that our baseline for communication should be misunderstanding. That is, we usually start with a misunderstanding and then struggle to achieve understanding. There is probably no clear-cut answer to the question of whether infants and mothers are naturally attuned at birth and become periodically disrupted, or whether attunement is an achievement of mutual effort. Nevertheless, it seems clear that attunement becomes a variable state between infant and caretakers, the developing child and his or her caretakers, and the adolescent and his or her world of later life.

We move on to the prerequisite for effective analytic therapy, which is to understand the patient. This is said to be ameliorative (if not curative) and necessary (if not sufficient, for any longstanding effect of treatment). In Kohut's (1971) concept, the process of treatment is characterized by a series of empathic connections or states of understanding followed by empathic breaks, which are then repaired by interpretation. This leads to his term for structure building: *transmuting internalization.* Thus, the meanings that are interpreted are those that have to do with the affective state or charge that accompanies feeling understood, followed by feeling a break in being understood, and the subsequent reestablishment of a particular merger, which Kohut considered equivalent to a state of mutual understanding. This last state is not merely that of the glue or holding previously discussed; the particulars of these transferences demand specific messages. So, too, the interpretations are designed to heal individual and therefore unique exchanges between patient and analyst. Yet the basic ingredient of this approach is a singular emphasis on interpretations that refer to empathic breaks and, in a parallel way, reconstructions that deal with similar failures in attaining and maintaining empathic understanding between parent and child. The integrated structure is ideally both stable and of a piece. It can, of course, be considered to have many shapes and forms and to connect with selfobjects according to different needs. The particulars of the connections yield the varieties of functions that we attribute to the self. It is here that we see the splitting of the structure that we consider another requirement in the constructed explanation of perverse behavior. As I demonstrate, the split is a result of, and is thus best seen as, the nature of the link to the selfobject.

The implications of Kohut's thesis are far-reaching since it is essentially a reduction of all psychopathology to a dysfunctioning self that comes about from empathic breaks. The nature of the disorganization, fragmentation, or depletion is a secondary phenomenon that is also of secondary importance because it is readily, albeit not easily, eliminated once empathy can be restored. For the moment, we can put aside the developmental progress that follows in an empathic environment as we concentrate on the pathological issues. If all psychopathology is the result of a less-than-intact system, we can assume that the system, once intact, can serve other functions that need not reflect a psychopathology per se. This says no more than that many kinds of communication can travel over the self-organization or between self and selfobject, that functions not related to self-regulation are not relevant to this state of disorganization, and that many meanings are exchanged that are not a part of mental illness. Although this sounds like using a computer model to demonstrate that intact hardware can run a variety of software, it is the least significant comment to be made about a self structure because there is no easy separation between structure and function. In this view, the different functions will come to be seen later, in the third level. I have separated, then, the levels of units and connections and so turn to the stories told during treatment.

The third level of concern has to do with the many types of representations the structure may manifest. If the train, its tracks, stations, and equipment are connected and running, then the system can deliver people, cattle, or grain, all of which are secondary to the railroad system. These particulars, as opposed to the elements of construction that we took as the first level, or building blocks, are of primary significance to many concerns of the railroad, but not to its operation or functioning per se. Nor are they the same as the operating capacity of the system. That exists, as noted earlier, as an overall form that sits between the elements and the representations. The meaning of specific representations not only occurs within, and hence is shaped by, an overall form, but must also be gauged with respect to the resulting understandability of the form itself. Thus, we build upon the state of understanding that we introduced with the self-selfobject link. At the risk of overstretching my analogy, imagine situations in which the train is late in arriving because of schedule problems, too many cars trying to use too few sets of tracks, or other problems akin to the dynamics of the situation. These phenomena may show what appears to be a conflict, but not as a result of any structural problem; rather, it has more to do with the ability of the system to manage the demands placed upon it. Conflicts do exist but are not coincidental with an inherent structural problem. Just as a conflict can be resolved by a reordering and redistribution of relative demands and capacities, we can say that an intact self can survive many conflicts without any sign of pathology—that is, with no sign of structural breakdown. Thus, the third level of meanings has to do with the many stories or narratives created during treatment. How it is that many theories of treatment are seemingly effective is answered by recognizing that the stories are more like epiphenomena than directly related to the formation of a symptom reflective of psychopathology. In a later chapter I explain that these interpretations affect a different level of achieving insight.

Most of what transpires in psychotherapy and psychoanalysis has to do with just those stories that come alive in the process. Although understanding a patient is essential, it is not the answer for everything. Kohut (1984) felt that the explanations that follow such understanding made a higher level of empathy possible. This proposition may do a disservice to the significance of the exchange of meanings. The explanations that follow understanding need a credibility of their own. Kohut probably wanted to emphasize the underlying structural component while minimizing explanations in his concept of cure. But the third level of meanings, the narrative exchange constitutes the major activity of most treatment, and it adds to the cure by allowing the achievement of a new function of self-reflection that may itself be likened to a mechanism of self-maintenance. The ability to think about and reflect upon one's relations to others is essentially the ability to explain to oneself what has been understood, and this capacity ensures the continuity and later development of the self. The stories are important; the meanings that are delivered are significant. Though perhaps secondary in the formation and persistence of the psychopathology, they are primary in the development and maintenance of the relations to the sustaining selfobjects. It remains our task to distinguish these levels and to seek empirical support for what makes for psychopathology and what is needed for its treatment. The story may, in turn, tell about the very need to maintain a connection and so doubly ensure the needed form of help. The third point of psychodynamics, then, is to add to the first, sexualization, and the second, splitting.

Illustration

This illustration aims to show the structure in a patient, one without perverse behavior, in an effort to generalize our approach to pathology.

Level 1: The Basic Connections

A female patient in analysis for several years showed a problem that recurred whenever she or the analyst took a vacation. She found herself apprehensive before the separation, but regardless of the particular pleasure or pain of the time spent apart she was always temporarily "out of synch" for several hours after their reunion. She remained in a state close to disorientation until some time, often several days, had elapsed. She felt strongly that she could not be hurried into resuming the normal work of analysis, nor could the analyst say or do anything to facilitate the reentry. He could, however, make it worse, as, for example, when he gave her appointment hours to other patients while she was away so as not to charge her for the missed times. This unnerved her because she needed to feel that the hours remained hers, that they were in place for her whether or not she was able to use them. Thus, when she had to leave the analysis for a brief period, she was much relieved to feel that her analytic hours would remain hers and not be offered, even temporarily, to other patients. No amount of scrutiny of her reaction to separation revealed any particular psychological aspect to this problem or to the solution of keeping the patient's hours open.

Here we have an example of a vulnerable person for whom the regularity of analysis shored up a fragility of the self. Such regularity is akin to the rhythms of exchange between mother and child but is inevitably more, since it is a part of almost every form of human relation—one usually taken for granted. Most people have enough of such basic connections to allow it to remain in the background, but they are essential to the further development and elaboration of the complex organization that is the self. This further development of the self is, however, seemingly affected by the action of the analyst rather than by insight and so is said to be not easily approached by a pure psychological intervention. I show later that this is a mistaken view of the limitation of interpretations. We have already seen how the sexualization that maintains connections is lifted by structuralization.

Level 2: The Self-Structure as a Basic Form

The patient over time developed a selfobject transference to the analyst that illustrated the emergence of an original, creative, and self-sufficient individual. Overcoming great resistances having to do with a multitude of somatic symptoms, she revealed a talent for writing that was stimulating to her but in perpetual need of validation that aided her in the regulation of her excitement; it was the formation of a mirror transference (Kohut 1971). This mirroring relation was seen to have been only temporarily emergent in childhood when the birth of a sickly brother had caused her parents to turn from her, at the same time asking that she not be any trouble so that they could tend to the new baby. The transference elaboration enabled her to have nascent exhibitionistic feelings understood. It also seemed to effect a transformation of a sometimes indecisive and uncertain person into a highly creative person who during periods of creativity could operate in an expansive and daring manner. Thus we saw that the particulars of the connection lent an added dimension to the self-organization vis-à-vis the sustaining self-objects.

This sketch of a form of the self is reflective of the mainstay of the work on narcissistic disorders. This particular self had one form and one transformation and so illustrated how the basic connections coalesce in the complexity of a self-configuration. The splitting we see in perverse behavior is another special and essential ingredient in perverse self systems.

Level 3: The Meanings

Here is the place for both psychodynamic explanations and historical validation. The patient was a poet who composed intricate and moving pieces that could be decoded to reveal the story of a lonely and neglected girl whose parents had little time for her. Some of the analysis had to do with filling in the story of her childhood; some had to do with dreams related to her wish for recognition of her talent; and some had to do with the construction of the product of her efforts, her poetry. Her history, her dreams, and her poetry were at one time or another all representations of the form of her self. If the patient felt understood, then the explanations that followed filled in her life's story, made sense of her dreams, and helped her better construct her poetry. Some of the explanations were about being able to be understood, following Kohut's basic premise that the disruptions of analysis lay the groundwork for interpretations. Meanings are, however, much more complex than this single line of empathic disruption, no matter if everything ultimately is reduced to it.

Some lines of her poetry were so rich in meaning that it would be a disservice to reduce them to this singular intent. The act of making poetry became the vehicle for self-reflection that allowed the patient to become free of the transference that had sustained her. The creation and exchange of meanings therefore allow us to understand ourselves and others. This is the story or the narrative of the dynamics or the childhood history behind the structure, and this is the richness of narrative that so often occupies stages in our treatments.

The overview of the structure of the self is designed as a paradigm for all therapeutic evaluations and interventions. It opens the door to the possibility that, at a minimum, psychopathology that responds to analytic treatment may pertain to the integrity of basic organization. If components of this organization are missing or feeble, then the treatment will have to be concerned with issues of regularity. If the self is defective, then the treatment will have to do with increasing the avenues of understanding. Here as well is the avenue of our connection to the world and to one another: the sense of reality. Decoding the many representations or manifestations of the self yields the dynamic picture that individualizes the structure. We must next tackle that crucial variable of the self: the split that divides it in two. It is the next ingredient of the threefold elements that make up a perversion. I have outlined the units and framed the structure and now continue to that crucial component: the vertical split.

4

A Certain Sort of Blindness

The split in the self leads to the convenient practice of disowning parts of the world that one finds disagreeable. Splitting, however, means many things to many people. To Phillip Manfield (1993, vii), "The essential character of splitting is that the person who is splitting has a distorted view of reality and in particular of relationships. He views himself and others (objects) in essentially all positive or all negative terms, black or white without gray. . . . His experience of the world is very different from that of other people." This viewpoint emphasizes the either-or phenomenon, slighting some salient other viewpoints, since not only does everyone split to some extent, but it is the coexistence of the terms of opposition that is the source of trouble, not the singularity of one or the other. The splits of psyches do indeed divide the world into a series of binary issues: castrated versus noncastrated, masculine versus feminine, alive versus dead, absent versus present, good versus evil, and so on. The lack of resolution becomes the problem. It is a temptation to reduce all the dualities involved to one essential point, such as castration, as Freud did, but that would be a false and arbitrary reductionism. It is also a temptation to make splitting fundamentally pathological and thus ignore the occasional advantage of the "suspension of disbelief" for many creative efforts.

Yet the most severe and costly temptation is to consider splitting to be a definitive or absolute exercise of division, ignoring the amount of splitting that occurs, from a temporary disregard of some reality to a long-lasting and severe insistence on the existence of a nonexistent state of affairs. We can see the spectrum from the process of coming to grips with the death of a loved one to the transsexual person who knows at heart that he or she is other than what may seem.

Entertaining a fantasy as we go about our daily lives is usually thought of as handling the frustrations, discontents, and needs of existence. Thinking about hamburgers, toilets, or sexual partners is a temporary device of delay until real satisfaction is achieved; imagining vigor, wealth, and beauty is a response to the temporary vulnerabilities and fears of everyday life. Usually, the fantasy is an innocent exercise. At times, however, it becomes a reverie, and we may become temporarily lost in exploring it. These incidents are splits, but the reality ego is ever ready to step in, correct, and certainly to curb action. At certain points in fantasy life, some material that is unpleasant, and possibly repressed, comes to the surface, and the associated unpleasant affect usually terminates the indulgence of daydreaming. Thus, negative affect alerts the reality ego to participate and so to turn its attention to the world as it is. However, at times the fantasy life remains so clearly divided from the life of reality that it seems to enjoy its own reality, and soon the possibility of action is brought into the picture. We see this in sexual life in the masturbation that accompanies a sexual fantasy. As the propensity to act goes into more broad-scale action, the fantasy may be realized. This realization demands a clear split from the more reality-oriented self, along with a cessation of any feelings of disgust or shame that might otherwise have brought the fantasy to a close. It is here that we see the coexistence of contradictory selves; it is here that the depth of the division is most dramatic. "In the narcissistic personality disorder (including, especially, certain perversions) we are not dealing with the isolation of circumscribed contents from one another, or with the isolation of ideation from affect, but with the side-by-side existence of disparate personality attitudes in depth, i.e., the side-by-side existence of cohesive personality attitudes with different goal structures, different pleasure aims, different moral and aesthetic values" (Kohut 1971, 183). Thus splitting takes on the definition not of seeing things as all-positive or all-negative but of living in two different worlds.

The Development of the Split

In considering the development of splitting we start with the premise that children are brought to the recognition of the varied realities of life and the world by way of parental mediation. Children determine what they are and who they are by affirming or rejecting the various beliefs of their parents. Parents regularly direct, modify, and control a child's perception. It is not only the little boy's sight of a person without a penis that leads to a split, but also the parents' communication about that state of affairs. The little boy who sees the castrated other does not inevitably attribute such a condition to himself. If he indeed does so, one wonders just why and how it had such an impact on him.

One telling example is that of a transvestite male who reports that his mother, before marriage to his father, gave birth to a baby girl fathered by another man. The illegitimately conceived child died shortly after being given up for adoption. Soon after, the mother married the patient's father, and they had a son. Years later, when the mother began a longing and reverie for the baby girl taken from her, the patient saw his mother as ever searching for that lost girl in him. He recalled her depression when he was a child and likewise recalled the experience of joy that came to him (and perhaps to her as well) when he was dressed as a girl by an aunt and later, when he dressed as a woman. His consideration of himself either alternatively or sporadically as man and woman seems likely to be a result of a divided vision of himself as now of one sex and now of another, a vision of mutual construction of parent and child.

A male heterosexual married cross-dresser reports episodes of dressing up in women's clothing whenever his wife is out of town. He sees his impulse to cross-dress not as a reaction to missing his mate, a feeling that he insists is absent from his life, but rather as a freedom to indulge in his perverse pastime. He would qualify, in Stoller's (1975) view, as a fetishistic cross-dresser rather than as a true transsexual because he appears masculine, enjoys intercourse, and thinks of himself as a man, yet has an unremitting fantasy of being an alluring woman. One day he brought photographs he took of himself in drag and was eager to know whether I found him attractive as a woman. Indeed, he wondered whether I would have simply assumed he was a woman had I not already known it was he. I felt uncomfortable. He looked like what he was: a rather burly male in drag. Nonetheless, I muttered something positive about how nice he looked in the pictures, which won a blissful smile from him. My having to affirm a reality that I felt patently false was not only a reassurance of support, it was more likely a reenactment in the treatment of parental participation in the construction of a nonexistent reality. The disavowal of reality that Freud noted in fetishism cannot be achieved by the singular activity of the child, but is a product of a mutually made-up world. The parent attests to the unreality needed by the child, the parent, and ultimately the patient the child becomes. (This is equally the case for the sudden appearance of a phobia that seems inexplicable: there is always parental participation.) Another cross-dresser tells of going shopping with his wife and his parents and standing outside a lingerie shop as the women go inside. His father laughingly asks whether he would like to go inside and try on a bra and panties. The patient experienced this moment with a shudder that seemed to resonate with an unremembered feeling of somewhere, sometime having been affirmed in femaleness.

McDougall (1978, 210) compares the pervert to the artist in the act of creation. She says that the artist offers his product for the judgment and contemplation by the public, while the pervert offers his to a secret relationship—"Basically an anal-erotic and anal-sadistic one between mother and child in the unconscious inner world." McDougall believes that the aim is to recover the confirmation of sexual identity and subjective value in the eyes of others. Indeed, the pervert has a greater need than the artist for the narcissistic confirmation and validation of his invention. She claims the role of the pervert's public is not to judge but to be duped. The sexual innovator for McDougall is a master of illusion, with a difference: "Art is the illusion of reality, an illusion that the artist creates for himself and for others in the hope that he may communicate and finally impose his illusion on others and have it accepted as such. The perverse scenario, with its specific plot and action, is the illusion that has imposed itself on the creator, but which he then, for the rest of his life, attempts to impose on others in the hope that they will accept this illusion as a reality."

My transvestite, however, does not impose his illusion on another to have it accepted as true, as much as he asks the other to "be of two minds," just as he is. He both quiets and activates the observer (even if he is performing in front of a mirror) to both know and not know. The illusion has imposed itself on the creator, but the wish is not to blind the other to reality but to cause the other to tolerate the two supposed realities; not to suspend disbelief permanently but to balance belief and disbelief; and not to embrace an unreal world but to satisfy the split in reality visited upon the child by the parent or parents, who lived in two worlds. Of course, the origin of the split may be lost in its later life.

Yet some acts of perverse behavior seem to reenact the early scenes of parental dualism in which the child and parent joined in the statement of separation. This is most notably seen during reenactments in treatment, when the patient attempts to communicate to the therapist how a split was demanded in order to stay connected to the parent, who was a sustaining selfobject. Over time such clear divisions can become obliterated or transformed into sequential behavior. An example is that of a perversion involving animals that seemed to occur in an excited period of anxiety and agitation and was followed by intense shame and humiliation. No doubt the reality ego was temporarily blinded during the performance, but the relationship with the animals did carry a meaning about the patient and his parents, if one could but read it. Still other forms of splitting have traveled so far from their origins that one is hard-pressed to find remnants of the negative affect that may once have accompanied them. Admittedly, these are rarely seen in treatment unless an external reality insists upon labeling the behavior as deviant. (Before much can be done to alter the behavior, such cases probably need what was once called an experience of being ego-alien; see chapter 9.) The point still holds that the split is a study in contradictions held by parent and child; its consideration is a requirement for effective therapeutic intervention.

Earlier I pointed out that children live with contradictions in early life, and so the chronology of splitting needs to be better located. For example, Melanie Klein suggests that the early defenses of the ego arise in the first year of life, a phase in which repression does not exist and in which the boundaries between the id and the ego are fluid. For Klein, primary splitting is necessary for survival. The baby splits her unconscious fantasies and anxieties related to her drives into absolute good and bad, absolute gratifying and persecutory breast, and so on. She can thus simultaneously project them outside and then introject them again (Steiner 1989). Thus we see the very earliest employment of the idea. The unlikelihood that these mechanisms operate at this early age is emphasized by Piagetian studies and conclusions about the child's capacities to perform certain operations. An even more radical suggestion is made by Mark J. Adair (1993), who posits the "creation" of body and motor hallucinations that serve to deny castration and other traumatic situations. The evidence against infantile hallucination is seemingly dismissed by the author (p. 83).

The cognitive development of the child must be correlated to what we know about the emergence of splitting, but it is simplistic to say that the onset of concrete operational thinking and the possibility for logical thought usher in the defense of disavowal at around six years of age (Basch 1988). In fact, recent work places it earlier, at age 3½ to 4 (Lewis et al. 1989). One way to deal with the cognitive line of development is to consider it as having a "nondefensive prehistory in the era of disparate self-nuclei before the secure establishment of a unitary, cohesive self" (Gedo and Goldberg 1971). This allows for the phenomenon of splitting to be explained as essentially a nonunification of the self, while actual disavowal forms by an active rift in the previously unified self to yield a new but distorted unity. The so-called synthetic function of the ego joins with the advent of concrete operations to yield a unitary self. Thus there may exist two forms of splitting: one that is more properly seen in borderline disorders, where the sense of unification is lacking, and the other in the varieties of narcissistic pathology, where unification is first achieved by the parents and later maintained by way of disavowal.

The active participation (or perhaps merely the presence) of a parent is needed for the achievement of unification, as outlined previously (Gedo and Goldberg). The active participation of the parent seems just as likely for the activation of disavowal. In one scenario, the parent assists in unification *until* the synthetic function and concrete operations arrive. The prehistory of disavowal is therefore one of parental failure to sustain the previously achieved unification. This perspective allows one to see that unification may be a task of both parent and child and that it is of variable quality. That is, all forms of unification are possible or potentially available by the simple process of omitting or discarding certain undesirable parts. The selection of such forms is initially unproblematic because the child can readily entertain contradiction; it is still not much of a problem later on when the parent becomes the mediator of reality. Once the child is able to practice splitting actively, the problem is once again solvable if not already partially solved. She knows a good deal about the self and the world and so ventures forth armed with that knowledge plus a capacity to segregate certain parts of an unacceptable world. The extent of disparity between the one and the other, the parental world, and the many new versions offered to the child lend shape to a newly constructed world formed by the many modifications and reconciliations demanded of her. That is why Freud (1940) emphasized the role of disavowal in handling painful or intolerable external percepts. The child is indeed the constructor of an acceptable world. Yet sometimes reconciliations are impossible, and the rift remains. It would be a different problem if splitting could be repressed and replaced by a neurotic symptom, but its conscious, periodic existence as a parallel sector is underscored by its appearance and coexistence. And the split sectors are ever in a search of particular affirming others who will support and validate what is to be taken as real. That is why splitting is part of a dialogue, one that represents a structure and can be seen as such in therapy.

There are thus many ways in which the developing individual shapes both himself and the world over time—at the same time as he searches for enduring connections. For many such constructions a split is needed. The evidence of the mutuality or reciprocity of splitting is inferred from the patient's history or is reenacted in the transference. Here is an illustration.

Case Illustration of a Split

The patient, whom I shall call Michael, is a young professional man who came for an analysis upon the advice of his psychotherapist, who had seen him for only a short time following an abrupt end to a previous analytic effort. Michael went to that first analyst following the breakup of a homosexual relationship. He was agitated and depressed and soon was also perplexed by the analyst's query as to whether Michael wanted his homosexuality to be analyzed or left alone. The patient's astonishment at the unexpected selectivity and precision of psychoanalysis soon gave way to a gnawing uncertainty about the competence of this particular therapist. In the midst of a series of unhappy and rancorous confrontations, he decided to break off the analysis and seek help elsewhere. Convinced that this first analyst was crazy, he sought therapy with someone of impeccable reputation and demeanor. The second therapist, however, acknowledged that an analysis was indeed indicated. This therapist, in a seemingly more fitting manner, answered the patient's question about sexual preferences with the assurance that one could be happy and well adjusted as a homosexual or heterosexual. In truth, as it was later revealed, the patient was best characterized as bisexual, an answer that offered him some relief. The second therapist was not an analyst and so referred Michael to me.

I saw my new patient. We agreed to start, and he soon wondered about my position on homosexuality. Was I for or against it? Could one be analyzed and remain homosexual? Would his homosexuality be a focus of the analysis? My general posture and demeanor could best be described as smug: I was so delighted by the ill-considered comments of his first analyst about the precise application of the treatment that I could reasonably employ several phrases to say, we will have to see what will be. In looking back, I believe my steadfast neutrality was essentially a result of my own bewilderment about the patient's questions. At that time, I had lost my once firmly held feeling about the pathology in homosexuality, and I no longer felt certain about the effect of psychoanalysis on sexual activity or sexual preference.

Michael is a slim, effeminate-looking person who dresses carefully, speaks clearly, and berates me unceasingly. The salient points of the case are familiar. Michael is the child of a domineering and dominant mother and a passive, barely remembered father. He has an older brother who hates the mother, hardly speaks to anyone, lives alone in another city, and seems to be more asexual than anything else. Michael was dressed as a girl by his mother when he was about four years old, was attracted to men early on, was seduced by an older man when he was in his teens, and declared himself to be homosexual while in college. He had a serious and intense affair with a homosexual lover of about the same age during graduate school, but sometime before that he had a fairly long-standing relationship with an older woman, with whom he enjoyed sexual intercourse. Michael's mother met and despised this woman, but she is now fairly accepting of his openly avowed homosexual orientation.

The matter of splitting and reality in this case starts with Michael's perception of my every possible fault and an eagerness to lambaste me every time a fault presented itself. I pride myself on doing things right: starting and ending on time, giving accurate bills, announcing vacations with adequate notice—trying hard to be the model of a modern psychoanalyst. Wrapped as I was in the self-assured cloak of neutrality and propriety, I could initially handle Michael's grievances with a calm air of detached yet empathic curiosity. But I began to falter.

My mistakes could have been overlooked, but they soon became featured stars. Sometimes I misjudged the clock, often I had to cancel and was accused of giving insufficient notice, and often I was heard talking to someone else in the halls. I began to worry about a compounding of errors. Michael told me that anyone who becomes an analyst has to give his work priority that did not allow for missed appointments, slovenly bookkeeping, or casual inappropriate conversation. As I comforted myself with the concept of Michael's resistance to a full-blown idealization of me, I suffered a parallel erosion of my own sense of competence and worth. I was becoming wary and irritable and subsequently tired of Michael. Of course, at times he seemed to appreciate me, and he certainly showed an impressive improvement in his symptoms, which had ranged from serious suicidal preoccupations to somatizing gastrointestinal maladies. He was getting better, but I was getting worse: primarily in Michael's view, but, inexplicably, also in mine.

One day I was speaking to my secretary, who sits in an adjoining office, about my plans to visit another city. Unbeknownst to me, Michael was in the waiting room. As soon as the hour began he launched into a tirade about my incredible lack of sensitivity in speaking loudly enough for him to hear, especially about something that would be important and even upsetting to him— my missing one or more hours of analysis. I began to mobilize a response. Michael went on and on. He sounded so sensible and rational. He then plaintively begged me to tell him why I lacked the good sense and decency at least to close the door when I spoke to my secretary. I felt I was going a little crazy and triumphantly blurted out that there was no door to close. That shut him up. Everything would have been fine, but I suddenly realized and even shuddered to recognize that, indeed, there *was* a door. I felt more than a little crazy. I felt trapped, and the next day Michael lost no time in accosting me with the undeniable existence of that dreaded door. I seemed to have no recourse but to lie and say that the secretary could not stand to have the door closed, so that at least functionally the door did not exist. I escaped, but at a price that shattered my smug and secure sanctuary of analytic detachment. I felt a little foolish and yet exhilarated because that rare moment of truly living out the transference had now captured the analysis. My own countertransference of cockiness and certainty, which surely covered my deeper anxiety about being just as incompetent as Michael's first analyst, had clearly been breached.

Michael and I had frequently discussed his split recognition of me: as a competent and trusted analyst and as a madman. We readily linked this to a similar awareness of his mother, who gradually emerged as a periodically psychotic person. There were memories of her becoming anxious to the point of derangement, of incredible rages against imaginary foes, and of unshaking convictions of wrongs that could never be righted. Yet alongside this was an equally clear vision of her as remarkably effective and reliable. The father could hardly be counted on for anything. Mother would and could accomplish it all, but often to the accompaniment of shame and humiliation for my patient. As Michael had left his first analyst, he regularly contemplated leaving me, but his tie to me as mother was unbreakable. Thus he became and remained a person of dramatic division, with an ego split that seemed to go beyond cognition to encompass the whole of his person, including his sexuality.

As Michael and I reconstructed his childhood life in two worlds, which he characterized as those of reality and craziness, he insisted that one was of his mother and one was of himself. With his first analyst, he was equally convinced that he wanted to hear exactly the silly words of assurance that his homosexuality would be left untouched and that he knew exactly what was going on. Just as Freud had said of paranoia: there is always a bit of us that seems to know just what is what. But what *is* what? Immediately after our reconstruction, Michael reported that for the first time in his life he felt "grounded in reality." He was relieved and convinced once again that I was the accurate representative and mediator of the world. Unfortunately, I was not equally sure of my own solidness.

Now for a dream. Michael is on a sailboat with his brother and mother; his mother is sailing the ship by pulling on ropes. Both Michael and his brother have similar rope-pulling tasks, but the brother is having a hard time. The mother goes to help, and the brother becomes angry at her interference. They struggle and fall in the water, and the brother drowns as Michael watches. Close upon the heels of this dream is another in which the patient wants to report his last dream to a group of people. He suddenly sees his brother in the group and so restrains himself from reporting the dream in order not to embarrass his brother.

These dreams had a certain clarity and consensus that contrasted sharply with other dreams that had previously prevailed in the analysis. The prominent focus of those earlier dreams was the plausibility of seemingly opposite interpretations. Of course, the overdetermination of dreams and symptoms makes this understandable, but Michael and I would often look at a dream and see how it could go either way. Usually the question centered on accepting one thing and ridding oneself of the other, and usually it was a debate between homosexuality and heterosexuality. I routinely chalked this up to the patient's ambivalence about his sexuality as well as about almost everything else in life. What haunted me at these moments, however, was the invitation for me to choose sides in the conflict, and I often felt an intense desire to resolve the issue according to what I preferred.

To return to the first dream, Michael and I agreed that I am the mother sailing the unsteady ship of analysis. Michael and his brother are the split parts of himself, representing the one that agrees with the mother (and me) and the one that disagrees and knows that she is in error. The brother is killed off in Michael's effort to resolve his split to join me in a hoped-for correct and unitary vision of the world: an integrated view of reality. Alas, this peace is short-lived, for it cannot ever be announced or proclaimed. Once again, in the next dream, the brother—the soul of disagreement—is alive, and once again, the analyst may be—and probably is—wrong!

Michael was upset with this interpretation, claiming that transference makes his life unlivable. How can he ever trust me? He has always known that I am a nut, yet has also had the unshakable knowledge that I am not. He can never relax his vigilance. He will never reach a point of rest, an end to this exhausting search of wanting and needing to know just what he is and what he should be. All his efforts to know what I think about homosexuality are intended only to position himself in terms of me, his mother, and the world. Resolving his transference is decidedly not a putting of one part finally to rest, since, in a peculiar way, they both make up his transference. In this same way, I suggest, they both—the sane and the crazy, the real and the unreal, the facts and the fiction—are a part of the world of all of us. When Michael is grounded in reality he is in possession of certainty, and he has that rarest of comforts. When he is victimized by the craziness of his mother or me, he is torn by an uncertainty that he knows is necessary for his survival. Complacency can never be his, since that is the road to submission and, for him, to oblivion. Putting himself together is a marriage of opposition, and he sees that only the obliteration of one part will enable him to feel unitary and settled; otherwise he will be doomed to uncertainty.

Splitting and Selfobjects

I postpone a discussion of the treatment and resolution of Michael's quandary and submit that the answer need not lie in the victory of one side or the other. Rather, it consists in filling in the gap, or what is sometimes called a defect. Such an obliteration of the split is often thought of as a form of healing, since it represents a need for the shades of gray proposed by Manfield. This effort consists of a union achieved by elements of gradation, but certainly at times such a gap seems almost impossible to bridge. The particular history of an individual such as Michael is a determinant of the nature of the reconciliation that is possible, and the case is a good example of the complexity involved. Michael is naive in thinking that his split occurs between his mother's view and his. His insistence that he saw and knew reality in spite of her is a conceit of folly, because the mother (and perhaps the father as well) was likewise the mediator of this alternate—and for him more correct—vision of the world. She was not always crazy, and so the simple picture becomes even more complicated because we must pick and choose from the many views offered to us by our caretakers and translators. This point needs underscoring because it is of direct significance to those analysts who claim that we must confirm the patient's personal perception of reality, inasmuch as a failure to do so obliges the patient to relinquish his sense of certainty in order to maintain an object tie. Since the world is always mediated and always constructed, any sense of certainty is the product of a construction and is never an absolute, direct perception. There is merit in the plea to try to see the patient's reality; the fault lies not in the effort but in the split. Since the world lends itself to different descriptions by different people, there can be no one true picture of the world. Every such description or vision of the world depends upon one or another object tie. Just as the parent is needed to unify the child's self in its development, so our selfobjects are needed to sustain and maintain us.

To return to my earlier discussion on delineating the levels of self structure, recall that the first level has to do with the building blocks of stability and manifests sexualization as evidence of fragility or breakdown. The second level has to do with the specific form of organization. This form, a stable configuration over time, is a product of connections between self and selfobject and, as I later illustrate, is a site for our study of splitting. The connection between the self and another, in this case a selfobject, is, in the cases we are studying, made possible by a separation in the self. One maintains a tie by necessarily turning a partially blind eye to some aspect of what one takes for reality. The split is therefore a vital part of the integrity of the self, and it carries on the unifying task that began in childhood by one's initial selfobject ties. Particular selfobject relations become the clue to what will be required to fill in the gap produced by the split. In an oversimplified scheme, one part of the self participates in a grandiose exhibitionistic display with an archaic or infantile selfobject, while another is oblivious to this behavior. This second or more realistic part has its own, more neutralized, mature, or perhaps repressed way of handling grandiosity— albeit unsuccessfully. The gap is bridged only by a selfobject that can do the work needed by each separate segment, a point I take up in the discussion of treatment.

The inevitable splitting of perversion takes place in an atmosphere of connections of special forms or types of relationships. The study of these connections is the place where empathy, the necessary medium of making connections, plays a vital role. That is why the effect to understand perverse behavior requires an entry point into the split off and sexualized sector of the self. Once this entry point is established, we can move to the next step in understanding the nature of an individual perversion: the psychodynamics peculiar to that individual and his or her life history. Splits are maintained by varying levels of effort, ranging from the feeling that another person exists who behaves in that way, to a puzzled feeling of wonder at where that behavior comes from, to an ever-present feeling of needing to hold it at bay. The explanation for the variety of such forms or levels of a split lies in the developmental program experienced by that individual, and so, necessarily, an effective treatment depends upon recognition of the nature of the gap and how it is maintained.

5

Psychodynamics and the Double Trouble of Perversions

The Study of Dynamics

A concern with dynamics has fallen somewhat into disrepute among psychoanalysts. What used to be a fundamental tenet of psychoanalysis, that "it explains mental phenomena as the result of the interaction and counteraction of forces" (Fenichel 1945, 11), has been eroded by a general waning of support for drive psychology and a lack of conviction that the truth can be obtained in terms of forces in opposition. Psychodynamics, in its heyday, was more than an expression of force and counterforce; it was an umbrella term for understanding the overall deployment of unconscious motivation (Alexander and Ross 1952, 28). In fact, according to one summary, dynamic diagnosis included: "(a) the environmental forces [involved] in precipitating or keeping alive a reaction . . . including the effect of certain neurotic attitudes of a parent on a child; (b) the internal, restrictive, permissive, punitive, and standard-setting forces of the personality, which go by the shorthand of 'superego'; (c) the instinct derivatives . . . spoken of as the 'id'; (d) the integrating, synthesizing, compromising, solution-forming, defense-creating aspects of the personality called the 'ego' . . . in contrast with the environment and with id and superego" (Levine 1952, 313). Although the psychodynamic diagnosis tended to include pretty much everything, it emphasized the unconscious. In this way it was distinguished from diagnosis based on genetics, which was also a story of the stresses and forces that mold the personality and thus also a matter of dynamics, though of times past. Therefore, for many of us, the psychodynamic formulation was an account of how the patient got to be where she was at the moment. Perhaps today we might present the narrative of that patient instead, since we are less certain that a diagnosis based on dynamics is much more than a plausible explanation.

Some stories are better than others insofar as they explain more, cover more ground, or are more coherent. One story offered by Joyce McDougall (1978, 59) propounds that all organized perverse formations contain essential features based on the oedipal constellation. For example, she says that there is a condensed primal scene in every perverse act. The various elaborations of the dynamics of this and other phenomena, including disavowal, serve to explain perversion. These explanations may differ from others, but the group as a whole supports Stoller's contention that just about every story works in diagnosing perversion. The story I offer here is not meant to be the definitive explanation, because no story is ever the whole story.

My story involves the development of the self, which comes about as a result of a complex set of relations. The data for laying out the patterns of the self come largely from the psychoanalytic setting, so the suggested forms of the self derive from observed self-selfobject transferences. Kohut (1971) has identified three such narcissistic transferences and has described how they can interact with one another: the mirror transference, based on a responsive selfobject; the idealized parental transference, based on an admired selfobject; and the alter-ego transference, based on an identical selfobject. These have been confirmed to be observable developmental progressions and regressions that become reactivated and can be studied in all analytic experiences. The unfolding selfobject transference is read as the self pattern reflective of a particular patient. The temporal sequence of its emergence in the analysis is a reflection of events in the patient's growth, although in reverse direction; that is, patients retrace self-development: what is seen first is what was last accomplished. For the self psychologist, the presentation of familial transferences is considered significant mainly in terms of selfobject functions because we study the pattern(s) of self-development, which we regard as built up from empathic bonds—first with parents, successfully or otherwise, and later with therapists.

These transference configurations are self patterns, and as they are followed over time, they allow us to say that the self is an enduring temporal and spatial system. It emerges at a moment in developmental unfolding when selfobject relations create a feeling of cohesion and consolidation, or the unification mentioned earlier. It moves along axes determined by innate programs and available selfobjects. It thrives in an atmosphere of sustaining selfobjects, and it suffers from the absence of nurturing others.

The particulars of self-development therefore vary according to the program, the talents, and the availability of the selfobjects. This variation can be seen as one of multiple adaptation, for a failure in one area can be rectified by turning to another. If, for example, the mother cannot mirror the child fully, the child can turn to the father for this function. Another variation of development is the trading off of one axis for another, so that a failure of proper mirroring can be handled by an emphasis on and greater investment in idealization. What follows from the multiple forms of adaptation is a mixed picture of a self: one more or less ambitious or idealistic, or ever struggling with weaknesses and vulnerabilities that were never fully able to be overcome or left behind, while constantly linked with those selfobjects that complement it or make it whole. Such a self uses selfobjects to complete itself and to handle deficiencies both defensively and by compensating as it further develops. Self pathology, on the other hand, has to do with the variety of such efforts and how they fail, including (1) a fragile self in need of shoring up by any and all available selfobjects, (2) a defensive self that covers over areas of defective structure, (3) an unfinished self that is unable to pursue further development because of a frozen relation with existing selfobjects. Together these make up the structure discussed in chapter 3.

Family Dynamics

The dynamics of psychological disorders are often described in terms of family dynamics rather than unconscious forces. Here there is a shift in the emphasis on causal factors from drive components to the influences brought about by the impact of the patient's parents. Stoller (1975) insists that perversion is the result of family dynamics that, by inducing fear, force the child who yearns for full immersion in the oedipal situation to avoid it. To him, perversion is "blighted heterosexuality" (p. xvii). Stoller's focus remains on the oedipal situation, but now he scrutinizes its failure.

As earlier noted, McDougall emphasizes the primal scene and describes the pervert as one whose mother holds an idealized place in his inner object world, while the father plays a negative role. McDougall makes a point of emphasizing the child's part in the "reinvented primal scene." She says that childhood magic is tailored to fit childhood desire and thus creates a "private erotic drama." In the evolving literature we see a subtle but distinct focus on what the child makes of his world rather than on what is done to the child, as in the statement, "The father, though usually present, is represented as an absence." McDougall's is a child-centered story. Chasseguet-Smirgel (1984) seems to incriminate the mother more in describing the parent as leading the child's ego ideal astray through "an insufficiency of narcissistic or object gratification, or through an excess of satisfaction" (p. 28). Morgenthaler (1980) likewise blames the parents when he says that the patient experienced all activities of parental figures as overwhelming and debasing sexual activities and that his comparison of these parental figures with himself was so disappointing and discouraging that a threatening sense of impotence and helplessness resulted. Socarides (1992) is unambivalent in describing the typical family constellation of a homosexual as consisting of a "psychologically crushing mother and an absent or abdicating father who does not assume his appropriate masculine role in relation to his son." The female homosexual views the mother as a malevolent and malicious figure and the father as one who does not respect his daughter's femininity. From this account one assumes that this view is an accurate one, and so the child is cast as a victim.

In the spirit of theoretical ecumenism, Kernberg (1993) describes a spectrum that begins with perverse features as components of normal sexuality, is followed by perverse features as components of neuroses, and moves to organized perversions. He then offers those perversions in borderline personalities to the British and French schools, whose dynamics are a condensation of oedipal and preoedipal conflicts under the dominance of preoedipal aggression. Sexual perversions in narcissistic personality disorders show the dynamics outlined by Chasseguet-Smirgel, which involve the full deployment of a regressive "anal universe." Kernberg speaks of patients whose early eroticism has not been activated and who have total inhibition of all polymorphous perverse fantasies, although it is unclear why these qualify as perversions. He ends by discussing homosexual psychopathology, but he seems equivocal on the existence of normal homosexuality. It likewise seems eminently clear to him that different dynamics apply to different perversions, but he remains puzzled as to why some people with these dynamics do not develop perverse behavior. Thus, we see a range of opinion that allows for oedipal and preoedipal problems and further differentiates perverse behavior on the basis of varied dynamics.

Selfobject Dynamics

If one posits the selfobject transferences as basic developmental themes, one sees the sexual life of the child in terms of three necessary connections: to a responsive selfobject, an admired selfobject, and an identical selfobject. Both gender formation and sexual focus require responsiveness from the parents. This need not be specific to the mother or father, save as each can respond positively or negatively. A negative response may lead to the formation of shameful and hidden aspects of both sex and gender. The admired selfobject likewise reinforces these self-images, and frustration here leads to a continual search for such an object to idealize and emulate. The parent who is not happy with his or her own sexuality lends a negative tone to the child's yearning and may foster a child who remains unfulfilled in valuing another. So, too, it is important to feel part of a larger group. Nothing seems to highlight a perverse activity so much as a feeling of alienation and difference; nothing seems to relieve it more than a feeling of acceptance, either in therapy or in a larger group. Thus the dynamics of self psychology clearly play themselves out in the understanding of sexual and gender differentiation and development.

A Clinical Example

I present a case that I reported on some years ago (Goldberg 1975) while I was developing ideas about sexual perversion. At that time I used it as an example of the sexualization of both the idealized parental imago and the grandiose self, together with the associated emotions that were replaced by sexual feelings. Although I am still convinced of that complex thesis, I have revisited my notes to see whether I could better understand the pattern of self-development I have described and so go beyond the variations on the oedipal theme.

The patient, whom I shall call John, was a divorced forty-year-old physician, the father of three. He had had a previous analysis. This treatment and the previous one were initiated by his being discovered in his perverse behavior, which took the form of fellatio performed on him by female patients whom he stimulated during routine physical examinations. The number of women who responded was unusually high, and John rarely repeated the behavior with any one of them. The behavior qualifies as perversion since it was episodic, associated with anxiety, and followed by what John described as guilt, but which was often clearly shame. The willing participants were unnamed and unknown and were no more than vehicles for the act.

John was one of six children reared in a small town by an extremely cold and religious mother and an alcoholic father. He recalls his mother as a demanding and unresponsive woman for whom the expression of emotion was a sign of weakness. His father became ill when John was a teenager and stopped working; he died several years before the analysis. The patient was unusually close to a brother who had died in an accident when a young man. The patient was markedly moved when discussing this event. An outstanding feature of the patient's childhood was an undiagnosed illness that began when he was eight and continued until he was sixteen. He had repeated intense pain in his right femur, which persisted for several days and nights and then would subside. The doctor could find nothing wrong with him and finally accused the boy of just not wanting to go to school. Thus John would endure pain silently night after night. He would often awaken, sit in his mother's chair and masturbate, sometimes while listening to the radio. Interestingly, no other member of the household was awakened during these activities, and the next morning the patient felt unable to tell his parents what he had endured the previous night. Finally, when John was sixteen, his older brother took him to an orthopedic surgeon who diagnosed a chronic infection of the bone and subsequently operated with complete success.

John reported that his deviant activities began after the birth of his first child, which was a boy. He began analysis shortly thereafter, when his perverse behavior was first discovered. That analysis concentrated on the perversion as a manifestation of a superego deficit. After a time the activity stopped and analysis terminated. The patient felt much better during analysis and was sorry that his symptom had returned rather soon after termination. He was hesitant to disappoint his analyst by reporting this event.

The second analysis began after his perverse behavior had been going on for several years. The patient reported it with extreme tension and agitation, and at times he was inaudible. John soon settled into a stable transference in which he longed to be a part of a strong, secure imago. The fellatio behavior illustrated to me the connection of a weak person to a powerful one. His partner in the behavior was represented in dreams as an old woman and seemed to be the weak, dependent image of the patient. He struggled to be the strong man with the big penis. The perversion subsequently diminished to the point of an occasional recurrence, which was seen as representing a disruption in the analytic situation. On one occasion, the patient's son became ill and needed surgery, and the patient canceled his appointment in anticipation of the procedure. An outbreak of his perverse acting out resulted, and dreams and associations revealed his struggle over a wish to ask the analyst to be available in case he was needed. The patient had a tremendous conflict over wanting to call the analyst to let him know what the surgery had revealed. He then recalled his overwhelming longing to tell his parents at the breakfast table that he had been in terrible pain the night before but clearly seeing in his mother's face that he had best not complain. He next remembered a tonsillectomy when he was four years old. When he was ready to leave the hospital, his father picked him up and carried him out. He had remembered this before with a feeling of outrage at being treated like a baby when he was old enough to walk out "like a big boy." But now, for the first time, John recalled how marvelous it had felt to be held securely in his father's arms and how he had longed for such a union with a powerful person. The perversion was now to be understood as mobilizing this very feeling of longing for union with an idealized and omnipotent figure, a feeling that was rapidly and effectively sexualized. In the behavior one sees not only the sexualization of the idealized parental imago—the sexualization of the grandiose self—but the experience of the feeling state as well, as sexual. Sexualization thereby overwhelms the structure along with the affect.

The story of John also can be a source of clarification about the precipitating event in adult perversions. The oft-repeated emphasis on "meaningful life events" (such as the birth of a first child in order to explain the onset of neuroses) is a phenomenological effort commonly given significance in nondepth psychologies. Interestingly, this patient, after long analytic work, revealed a combination of situations involved in the outbreak of his perversion, of which his son's birth was a rather minor factor. In particular, he was about to embark on a career that would necessitate his being a central and important person for long periods. John's agitation and excitement became almost unbearable; they were partially handled through his perverse activity but were more adequately resolved when, during his first analysis, he chose to pursue a different specialty. Only during his reanalysis did he reexperience those upsetting feelings and decide to begin again on his original specialty. The birth of his son contributed to the problem by making the patient's wife less available as an object to absorb some of his exhibitionistic fantasies, but this patient's problems were narcissistic, and he needed self-objects to handle his tension. This explanation is in distinction to that of conceptualizing competitive or hostile feelings toward a rival son.

Recapitulation

My effort to follow the development of a stable transference configuration showed the concurrent operation of two deficits in John: first there would be an upsurge of grandiosity—say, an excited feeling about some accomplishment, such as being accepted in medical school; next there would be a beginning sexualization. The patient's effort to hold this in check led to fatigue and irritability, which soon became associated with memories of his loss of his fundamentalist religion when he was an adolescent; that is, the religion had served as a temporary suppressant. During analysis this search for a selfobject replacement was seen in a dream picturing the analyst as a clown. Soon thereafter, the patient remembered that when he was seven years old his father was hospitalized and that he was devastated without his father. This seemed to echo the wish for and failure of a source of enduring strength and admiration. What seemed to be representative of the case was a beginning grandiose relationship with the mother, which failed, followed by a turn to idealization of the father, which, although partially successful, also came to grief. As the analysis proceeded, much of the work on exhibitionism and grandiosity, as evidenced in his showing himself and his accomplishments to me, seemed to be an answer to the perverse behavior, but there was always an accompanying wish to apprentice himself to a teacher or tutor, to reconnect with the lost father. Now again the sexualization might break out. Work on both poles—grandiosity and idealization—was needed as a response to the sexualization. Perhaps, since the perversion was so closely linked to sexual exhibitionism, it could be seen as primarily a defect of grandiosity, with no sign of a gender problem. The turn to the father was a partial answer, but that also remained unsatisfactory.

No doubt I did not follow or understand this patient adequately, but as I saw more cases of perversion, I became convinced, along with Kohut (1977), that all the patients had problems of self-development at both poles and that they all had chronically unstable lives. With some exceptions (which I detail later in this chapter), they did not seem to join adequately with the selfobjects of their world to complete themselves over time, that is, to achieve a sense of unification. In contrast to this chronic instability, many other forms of narcissistic pathology, such as empty depression, do seem to have achieved a relatively unifying experience with existing selfobjects, although at the price of a different order of symptom. Behavior disorders, such as perversions, manifest sporadic episodes of action that reflect an oscillation between the poles of organization and an inability to resolve tension. On occasion, a more or less regularized form of behavior emerges as able to effect unification, but most perverse behavior—or at least whatever continues to define it as perversion—has an episodic occurrence preceded or followed by shame or anxiety.

Although we may posit the origin of sexual and gender affirmation in that time of awareness of the genital zone, the pleasure or pain that ensues when this is carried into sexualization has a change in character that removes it from that focus on affirmation. The specific activity of sexualizing is used to handle the feelings associated with narcissistic injury, namely, the failure of a selfobject. That activity soon becomes available for the management of feelings that cover various situations, and the success of sexualization thereupon becomes the obliteration of feeling itself. Thus, the negative affects that were originally part of the vertical split—disgust and disbelief—are caught up in the sexualizing activity, and nothing of moment save pleasure is felt during the perverse behavior. In this way, all sorts of intense and potentially distressing feelings can be handled by sexualization, which soon moves away from the original context of occurrence to one that seems to bear no connection to sexuality as such. An example of such nonspecific action occurred when John acted out shortly before I was to return from my vacation. He confessed that he had missed me and was excited about my return. He associated this with a memory of being afraid to see his Christmas presents and of anticipating becoming unbearably excited. He next recalled a similar fear of excitement at the anticipation of his father's return after a long absence. He now felt a combination of guilt and apprehension at our getting back together. Although one may read several meanings into this sequence of events, fundamentally this shows a true psychoeconomic imbalance: a nonspecific way to master feelings.

Sexualization is thus employed as a generalized tension regulator, and so it need not reflect a particular dynamic conflict of the moment.

We are all familiar with the displacement of specific feelings to the sexual arena, as in the hypersexuality that follows or accompanies bereavement. This is essentially the basis of the handling of almost all emotions in the perversions. It is not uncommon in many cases of sexual perversion that a dearth of emotionality coexists in much of the patient's life. What may often be expected as an affective response is handled in the sexual sphere. To understand the nature of the psychoeconomic imbalance and the obliteration of affect better, we need to focus on the fragility of the self.

The Concept of Narcissistic Vulnerability and Faulty Drive Regulation

Kohut (1971) first attributed the failure of the psyche to maintain narcissistic homeostasis to a disturbed relation with the idealized object. That is, the parent responsible for the smooth regulation and handling of the tensions and disequilibrium of everyday life, usually the mother, is able to tune in to the varying needs of the child to establish periods of calm and ease. Failures of the parent in this regard led to the restless, irritable, hypersensitive patients who rarely enjoy such periods of peace. Later (but still preoedipal) difficulties led to an inability to control and regulate the drives and allowed for the appearance of sexualization.

For individuals with narcissistic vulnerability, the entrance into sexual life at the oedipal period is both a challenge and an opportunity. The particulars of idealization and grandiosity are played out in the sexual differentiation of the child. If the child once again confronts a parent unable to respond to the needs of that developmental period, a new set of damage to the self is experienced and superimposed on the earlier one. The extent and depth of the split are also much dependent on the earlier structural deficit, and Freud's emphasis on castration and the resultant belief in the phallic woman, based on disavowal of the absence of the penis in women (Freud 1927), is predicated on a weakened structure able to be so torn apart. John had a split, but it was displayed in terms of his grandiose exhibitionist sector and had to do with segregated images of himself as powerful, with no gender disorder whatsoever. His greatness was in the service of curing and healing a depressed mother, and this was ultimately expressed in a crude sexualized manner. His partial failure of idealization with his father as an answer to his defect threw him back on his unsuccessful mirroring by his mother, but it strains the theory if one tries to posit a phallic mother as also contributory to the problem. One can more profitably explain the dynamics without that addition. Similarly, Kohut (1971) sketched a case of a perverselike disorder (with no active sexual behavior) by postulating the need for an idealized father imago represented by fantasies of pursuing powerful men and a possibly unconscious fellatio fantasy (p. 72n).

Such failures in parental participation to enable the child to achieve homeostasis, of course, are due to the admixture of the infant's needs and the nonresponse of the parents. One must echo Kohut's (1971, 65) position that the major fault lies with the mother in projecting her moods to the child, overresponding, or failing to respond. This chronic lack of empathy results in the shaky structure attributed to the first and second levels of the self structure, regularly a result of the mother's misalliance with the child. Therefore, when one begins to assess the dynamic disorder in certain individuals, it is often the case that one or another negative appellation is assigned to the mother. True as this may be, it may be profitable to note that this failure of the mother is often translated into the diffuse vulnerability seen in the patient's handling of the tensions of everyday life. So, too, the failure to experience and tolerate affects is a measure of the general fragility of the self. Gradations of emotionality depend on the structuralization which is a result, at a minimum, of the mother's responsiveness to the needs of the child during the earliest moments of tension regulation. The further failure of idealization by the parent leads to a lack of the structure building needed for controlling action and affect and allows for the sexualization that overwhelms the self.

I am convinced that all perversions suffer to some extent from diffuse narcissistic vulnerability, which to varying extents participates in the sexualization experience. This may well be the basis of the affect disturbance in perversion, and it may also be a problem with a wide range of potential disturbance, a problem that is potentially quantifiable. All the sexual dynamic problems are of necessity superimposed on this fundamentally fragile structure. To this I later add the component responsible for sexual activity per se, that is, the distinction between action and fantasy without action.

The swing from one pole to the other reflects the underlying diffuse narcissistic vulnerability and the failure of adequate structuralization of either pole during the oedipal period. To say, as does Anna Freud, that the component parts of sexuality are not subsumed under a final common pathway of heterosexuality does not fully explain several not uncommon phenomena. One is the coexistence of perverse behavior and heterosexuality; the other is the routine role of heterosexuality as itself an activity to handle overstimulation and regulate tension. One may, of course, postulate an underlying unconscious fantasy operant during "normal" intercourse, but such acceptable sexual activity often serves to reinforce a temporarily weakened self. At such times, the dynamics become inconsequential, and to see the sexual activity representing one or another family scenario is irrelevant and secondary.

This reading of the problems of perversion may convey the impression that the perverse are the ones having all the conceivable difficulties. A disclaimer is in order. Thus far we have seen that the disorders of perversion have a vertical split and that the extent of the split varies. The split allows the perverse sector to operate as if it were a separate personality and thus permits a distortion of reality from mild to extreme. It is present in all perversions, probably has no good or clear correlation with the general psychological health of the reality sector (as Glover noted), and, as we shall see, needs to be focused upon separately in treatment. The second requirement is that of a defect in idealization, which allows for the sexualization. (In the chapter on treatment I try to pinpoint the developmental problem.) Insofar as the emotional life of these individuals is caught up in the sexualization, an overall narcissistic vulnerability seems to exist as well. This is by no means specific to perverse behavior disorders. In the arena of psychodynamics we are able to scrutinize the particular forms that lead to perversion, and, in my experience, both narcissistic poles (or, including twinship, perhaps all three) are involved because of the incredible variety of sexual scenarios that represent perverse behavior. More clinical material may better explain or alter that conclusion.

A Clinical Example

Richard is a patient with homosexual voyeuristic fantasies who returned to analysis after a weekend during which he was intensely preoccupied with looking at men's penises in the locker room at his gym and in various magazines, which he purchased with great shame. He also reported that he had enjoyed sexual intercourse with his girlfriend coincident with this upsurge of voyeuristic fantasies. He was tense and cautious during his analytic hour and paused frequently, as if to allow or even invite the analyst to talk. He reported a dream of a woman telling him things while simultaneously cutting him with a knife. He connected the dream to the analysis, in particular to a session some days earlier when he recalled that the analyst had coldly asked him to associate to a dream and not to try to read the analyst's mind. The patient had responded quickly that it was painful to experience the analyst's coldness. The analyst realized (but only to himself) that what he had said was hurtful. It was talked about for several sessions afterward and was brought up again by both patient and analyst in terms of the dream as illustrative of analytic interpretations as being cutting though accurate. The patient next talked of trying hard not to be so sensitive, to act and be tough in spite of all the things that hurt him. He had long known and felt that he had to guard against inadvertent injuries from friend and foe alike, and now the analyst joined those ranks. With each injury there came an associated question about what the person really thought of him. A movement away from the traumatic relation with the analyst-mother of the dream to a yearning for a safer connection to the father is now seen as expressed in the search for the strong penis that will protect and shield him. With this exploration comes the intense curiosity to read the analyst's mind, to find out what the analyst really thinks of him, and to unlock the secrets of the father, who seemed to be safe himself but seemingly could not lend that security to the child. Once again, the to-and-fro dynamics play out on an essentially vulnerable self. Both poles are involved, and the general weakness of the self prevents the full experience of feeling. The dynamics are decipherable but hardly form a sufficient explanation.

In a sense, the dynamics are epiphenomena. They are there, and they are interesting, they make sense to the patient in terms of his or her life's history, but what matters is the underlying structure. In addition to a basic narcissistic vulnerability are the dual problems of grandiosity and idealization, neither of which has been successful in stabilizing the self. Each parent fails in his or her own way, and the particulars of the failures lead to the variety of phenomena that characterize perversions. The persistence of the perversion usually bespeaks the ever-present defect of the self, which is repeatedly manifested by sexualizing activity aimed at a restitution and solution of sorts. Yet the sexualization sometimes seems to work, in that it does more than offer a temporary balm: it lends itself to a clearer and more definite feeling of unification. It lives a life of its own, and that is what I turn to next.

In summary, there may well be specific forms of dynamic forces and family dynamics for different perversions, with a clear correlation between, for example, pedophilia and one form of dynamics, and between shoe fetishism and another. It is unlikely, however, that one form of dynamics fits all, and it is highly unlikely that a specific form will have an inevitable outcome. The bigger question is why so many people with those same dynamics do not become perverts. In investigating a specific form of sexuality (homosexuality), I concentrate less on the dynamics, which may well be specific, than on that quality which makes it a perversion (sexuality) and a solution that may release it from that designation.

6

Homosexuality as a Compensatory Structure

The title of this chapter demands two definitions. Although one may assume that everyone knows what homosexuality is, it is necessary to clarify the term as well as that of "compensatory structure." Richard Friedman (1988) lists four behavioral components of homosexuality: erotic fantasies, sexual activity with others, a perceived sense of identity, and social role. These may exist together or singly, and none is a definitive standard for homosexuality. One cannot help but be impressed and even troubled by the absence of a uniform methodology for explaining how these components—which range from private musings to public performances—function.

The idea of a compensatory structure comes from the discipline of psychoanalysis, particularly self psychology. That theory says that patients in psychoanalysis demonstrate a certain configuration, a certain set of phenomena, and a certain transference that is often, but not always, representative of a special kind of disorder. My aim is to link this transference configuration to homosexuality, but I begin the task by restricting my inquiry and my evidence to the analytic situation. The data base of psychoanalysis must remain the source of study, since much of the unhappy status of homosexuality derives from the strained effort to cram social and interpersonal issues into the frame of the intrapsychic.

Kohut (1977) defined a structure as compensatory when it compensates for a defect of the self. In contrast to a defensive structure, which mainly covers over such a self-defect, a compensatory structure succeeds wholly or partially in a functional rehabilitation of the self. Kohut, at that point in the development of his theory, offered two poles of self-development: grandiosity and ambition versus idealization; he also suggested that the self-esteem of ideals of one pole usually, but not always, compensates for a weakness in the other pole of ambitions and exhibitionism. Nonetheless, elaboration of the basis for considering a structure as compensatory rather than defensive demands supporting theses, since one cannot assume that any given behavior or personality trait deserves to be called one or the other. In drive psychology it is assumed that all defenses are compromise formations, but that phrase has been so extended (Boesky 1988) that one would be hard pressed to define a compensatory structure except as a variant of such a compromise. Perhaps one could consider a compensatory structure as one composed of neutralized energy, to carry the meaning that this structure had become free of conflict. We need, instead, to invoke a description of the structure as operating, like neutralization, in a manner that is functionally efficient and free of regression of any pathological significance. A compensatory structure is therefore a solution rather than a temporary respite. It must be effective in its own right and not operant primarily to protect against other problems and potential difficulties. So when we say that a compensatory structure covers over defects, it must be in the sense that the defect is for the most part silenced as opposed to the persistent clamoring representative of and within a defensive structure. The gratification and pleasure of the functional operation of a defensive structure is indeed at least partly so in quieting the underlying defect (in the structural sense) or conflict (in the drive psychology lexicon). The gratification and pleasure of the functional operation of a compensatory structure lie more in the full operation of the coherent self in the activity. It is not an ego function that has gained autonomy, since it represents a cohesive personality organization. As such it no longer bespeaks or represents the defect or vulnerability out of which it originally came to be. Such a functional operation must once again be primarily considered in a psychoanalytic sense, in that it may well be that a cohesive and firm activity of the self leads in turn to a variety of social pressures and mishaps.

The concept of compensatory structure was employed by Kohut (1977, 193) to clarify the difference between narcissistic personality disorders and narcissistic behavior disorders by an example of similar dynamics in a man leading in one case to sadistic behavior toward women and in another to sadistic fantasies. Although each man was judged to have similar defensive structures, one had achieved enough compensatory structure to inhibit the fantasy effectively and so to experience narcissistic imbalance by way of autoplastic symptoms. We thus can construct a spectrum of self-development that allows for the wide deployment of relationships with selfobjects and can therefore lead to an array of normal selves, ranging from the highly ambitious—those who rely primarily on mirroring selfobjects— to the very idealistic—those who seek mainly to merge with an omnipotent other. The varieties of the normal self are not to be judged on the appraisal of that person's apportionment of one or another pole of the self but rather upon the capacity to sustain relationships with selfobjects and so to function in a fully cohesive manner. Psychopathology occurs when there is a developmental defect that is defended against and not fully compensated for. As Kohut (1977, 58) also illustrated, the psychoanalytic treatment of many narcissistically damaged patients is often directed toward a rehabilitation of the compensatory structure, by which the failure of one pole is made up for by the development of the other. Thus we may have: (1) a normal self with a varied distribution of grandiosity, idealization, and twinship, or (2) a narcissistically damaged self with either (a) grandiosity compensating for failure of idealization or vice versa, or (b) grandiosity defending against idealization or vice versa.

If the compensation is effective, there is no evident psycho-pathology, since there may be only a limitation on the self in terms of the breadth of the individual's experience. If the compensation is only partially effective, we see evidence of a narcissistic personality disorder. If the compensation fails, we see evidence of a narcissistic behavior disorder. In all these psychic organizations, we also note effective and ineffective defenses. I turn now to a group of sexual behaviors that lay claim to the position of an effective compensatory structure, all the while being misunderstood as being true perversions. It is important that the psychoanalyst separate the effectiveness of a compensatory structure from its interpersonal consequences. For that distinction, I turn to the illustration of homosexuality, since there is no doubt that the social status of homosexuality is problematic at best.

The Literature Reviewed

There is an enormous literature on the subject of homosexuality. The topic is met with general unease in psychoanalysis. The statement in the 1983 American Psychoanalytic Association (APA) Glossary reflects what may be taken as an official position:

In the male homosexual there is, as a rule, an overly strong attachment to the mother up to and including the oedipal phase, which is not resolved by identification with the father but rather by partial identification with the mother. Object choice is narcissistic in type, i.e., the loved person must be like the self, and sexual excitation is experienced in regard to men instead of women. Due to strong castration fears, the homosexual man cannot tolerate a sexual partner without the tremendously valued male organ. Another common motive for homosexual object choice is the avoidance of rivalry with fathers and brothers.

In female homosexuality the woman retains a strong original pre-oedipal attachment to the mother, which is displaced onto the homosexual partner. As a result of an unsatisfactory outcome of oedipal conflicts, her identification with the mother is incomplete and she holds onto mother as an object of love. (Moore and Fine 1983)

A dramatic change in this position is underscored in a panel report of the American Psychoanalytic Association (1986) in which the panelists were of one mind in depathologizing homosexuality, at least in the male. Stanley Leavy feels that an essential component of homosexuality is innate and that no influence or experience can bring about a final common pathway of homosexuality without this core. Faced with the evidence of widespread homosexuality in prisons and other situations in which opposite-sex partners are unavailable for prolonged periods, one would suppose that Leavy would qualify his position. Richard Isay has presented clinical material that mitigates against any effort to induce homosexual men to become heterosexual (1989). He has also stressed the preference of homosexual men to be treated by similarly oriented analysts or therapists. This does bespeak a tendency to politicize partially what is ideally a scientific problem. The nonscientific status of psychoanalysis is underlined in this panel by Stoller, who suggests that there is no such thing as homosexuality and that we should start the inquiry afresh. Although his far-ranging view of the matter is best thought of as exhortative rather than informative, Friedman is certainly the most informative both in the panel and in his later book (1988), where he urges that all aspects of homosexuality and heterosexuality be considered. His final chapter presents a hierarchical model and echoes the point made in Gedo and Goldberg (1971) that "in certain situations, regression to more archaic modes of organization may occur, but functions that have attained autonomy from conflict may not participate in returns to mere primitive positions." Friedman notes this to explain what happens to men with either differentiated homosex-

ual or heterosexual fantasies who experience severe psychopathology while their sexual fantasies remain unchanged. I
should like to modify this application to suggest that the rehabilitated compensatory structure has gained an autonomy that
forces us to reconsider the concept of homosexuality and psychopathology less from the point of view of a particular symptom or symptom complex than from that of the totality of the self
in operation. This is also suggested by Friedman, who says that
erotic fantasy or homosexual imagery cannot be understood in
terms of psychoanalytic theories of drives and conflict but must
be considered as "a structural part of the core self-concept." If
this is true for erotic imagery, it may well profit psychoanalysis
to consider the many variants of homosexuality in terms of self
psychology.

Clinical Considerations

As I have noted, the transferences that develop in the analytic
treatment of disorders of the self reflect the developmental program that has been pursued by the patient to a maladaptive
result. The studied poles of self-development—grandiosity, idealization, and twinship—become the dominant configurations
of the analytic transference. Any individual will manifest some
configuration of these poles in his or her final self system, and
the psychoanalytic treatment of that individual will, for the
most part, concentrate on the weaknesses and inadequacies of
that system. This comes about, as in any analysis, by way of the
patient making an assignment to the analyst: an assignment to be
a particular person, to take his or her place as a particular selfobject, or to perform a particular psychological function. The assignment then, over time, represents the stable narcissistic transference that presents itself for resolution through interpretation.
The assignment necessarily has the impact of restricting the analytic work to the particulars of that patient's program. This is
illustrated by Michael, the patient discussed earlier who was
asked by his first analyst whether he wanted to have his homo-

sexuality analyzed or left alone. Aside from its sheer silliness, such a question highlights the fact that the analyst is constrained to allow the transference to unfold without interference. He or she has no choice (Stolorow and Trop 1993).

For most patients who come for an analysis of self disorders, the psyche is not neatly divided into sick and healthy parts so that a successful analysis of the predominant structural defect results in an integrated self. Yet, as emphasized by Kohut (1977) and noted above, perversions in particular (Goldberg 1975) seem regularly to show defects in both poles of the self, and the resultant sexualization cannot easily be reduced to either a basic structural defect or the effort, though unsuccessful, to compensate for that defect. The sexual activity of most perversions is, however, characteristically directed to maintaining a relationship to a sustaining selfobject by active mastery, one devised to manage the potential disruption of selfobject equilibrium. The structural defect is filled in by the sexual activity, which, of course, may range from the most bizarre behaviors to what appears to be perfectly ordinary heterosexual intercourse. Again, the behavior is never an accurate indicator of the problem.

In the three cases of male homosexuality noted below there is a clear presentation of sexualization. Although an astute diagnostician would readily characterize these cases as instances of sexualization, the characterization is primarily, if not exclusively, dependent upon the outbreak of the activity that reflects the vicissitudes of the transference. There may exist cases in which sexual activity is not relevant in the treatment, and although such cases seem foreign to the basic concepts of psychoanalysis, they may be widespread. In the cases under consideration, however, the sexual behavior had a place in the transference and so was subject to psychoanalytic scrutiny.

Case One

Roger is a forty-two-year-old biology professor who came to analysis because his homosexual activity was getting out of control. He was frightened by the intensity of his needs and the potential risks of his escapades, not the least of which was the possibility of contracting AIDS. He regularly frequented gay bars but had also had occasional long-standing homosexual affairs. He did not have an obviously effeminate appearance, and he expressed a strong wish to be straight.

As a boy he was intensely close to his mother and only inter-mittently close to his father, who was divorced from the mother when the patient was seven years old and thereafter visited his son only sporadically. The patient was torn between his mother and father, who bore animosity toward one another until the father's death. The sexual life of the patient was primarily homo-sexual with erotic fantasies of men. He dated and enjoyed being with women but had not had successful intercourse with a female.

The analysis was primarily that of an idealizing transference. The erratic sexual behavior that characterized the patient's en-trance into treatment slowly subsided as the transference took hold. The particulars of his sexual escapades had to do with sadomasochistic positions and maneuvers that seemed mainly to represent issues of control of the inevitably disappearing self-object. The diminution and disappearance of these behaviors in treatment were accompanied by an intense wish to be heterosex-ual. All the other areas of the patient's life improved, but he seemed unable (though not unwilling) to become sexually in-volved with a woman, even though his nonsexual female rela-tionships were significant and meaningful. He terminated his analysis with a sense of having accomplished a great deal, along with a clear feeling of a limitation to his being any different in terms of sexuality.

As a result of the analysis of the idealizing transference, the patient developed a renewed vigor and interest in his life's work. His self was primarily organized along the idealizing pole, and the underlying problems of the grandiose, exhibitionistic pole were not and could not be engaged in the analysis. This pole, constructed around showing oneself to an admiring and mirroring selfobject, was the most damaged of the three cases. The idealization seemed to compensate for the damage and itself showed a weakness that was handled by a sexualization that was homoerotic. Once this pole is rehabilitated, the self may well be restricted to this form of sexual pursuit. Only when this pole does not serve as a compensatory structure can we reasonably expect the emergence of heterosexuality. Thus, in this case, the compensation worked so well that it rehabilitated the self. We see the patient as no longer needing to sexualize but also unable to be sexual other than in a homosexual manner.

Case Two

The second case is a reconsideration and revision of a case I reported on some years ago (Goldberg 1988). At that time I struggled with the fact that a seemingly successful analysis of the patient, a man who considered himself to be primarily homosexual, had not resulted in a definitive sexual orientation for him.

Jan is a homosexual man who entered analysis primarily because of his unhappiness over homosexuality and his longing to be heterosexual. He presented a blatant case of someone who did not fit in: he refused to belong to any sort of homosexual group yet could not bring himself to identify with heterosexuality. His sense of being "neither fish nor fowl" had its origin early in his life and went far beyond his sexual proclivity. Born into a blue-collar family of high-school graduates, the patient was an only son, with one older and one younger sister. Jan had an outstanding college record and became a professional. He seemed different from his family in almost every conceivable way. His father, who worked in a factory, was gruff, drank beer, and watched television. Jan loved music and fought with his parents to take violin lessons. He was bookish, sensitive, and totally at odds with the interests of his family. His mother is still not certain what Jan does in his work, and she has an air of not quite believing that he is indeed her son.

The mother's difficulty in accepting her maternity seemed to have been an issue early in Jan's life. She seemed chained to her own mother, who was clearly overtly psychotic and always present in Jan's home. The patient's mother had little time for her son, and Jan was always fearful of his grandmother. He knew that he was intruding on the relationship between her and his mother whenever he wanted a little time and attention from his mother. He recalled being sent off repeatedly to play at the early age of about four years, when this was hardly his desire. Sometimes he would go upstairs to a neighbor's apartment to talk or to sit in the kitchen with her. Jan was a thin boy until about age seven and a half, when this neighbor moved away, and he then began to eat a great deal. Although his younger sister was born at about this time, he later insisted that he felt the eating change was due not to her birth but to his having nowhere to go and no one to talk to. Overall, Jan recalled being anxious all through his childhood and strongly insisted that no one had supervised him or paid much attention to him. It was evident in the transference, however, that he felt that only certain aspects of himself merited attention, while other parts of his personality were best ignored. This was the grandiose pole that seemed difficult to engage in the analysis.

Jan's sexual history paralleled some of the key points of his life. He recalled the age of four as the time he looked at and touched little girls and the age of eight as the time he began homosexual activity by grabbing and feeling other boys. He described how a classmate in grammar school had later involved him in mutual masturbation. He said he was afraid to tell the teacher and unable to resist the advances of the other child. He masturbated regularly and continually throughout high school. Later in the analysis he revealed that as an adult, masturbating or going to a pornographic movie was an almost daily occurrence. Jan was shocked when he came to realize the consuming nature of his sexual preoccupation.

Apart from the mutual fondling that occurred in grammar school, which lasted only a short time, Jan's first homosexual behavior did not occur until he was approximately twenty years old. His first experience was not a pleasant one, but he soon became involved with a young man who was his lover for several years before he started analysis. Shortly before treatment began, their sexual life became meager, and they drifted apart soon thereafter. The patient was unable to visit homosexual bars because he felt horrified at the idea of being identified as a homosexual. His sexual orientation was known to only a few close friends.

During the beginning of analysis, Jan revealed another form of sporadic sexual behavior. This consisted of going to a place in the park where several men congregated nightly for flagrant, anonymous, and abbreviated sex. The people so totally lacked involvement that no one knew or cared who was doing what to whom. Jan was a completely passive sexual partner throughout these episodes, which filled him with disgust, yet he periodically felt drawn to the place. This passivity seemed to be a sexual display of his need both to remain aloof and to struggle against more meaningful involvement.

He described his family in bitter terms, with the exception of his older sister, who lived in California and whom he visited periodically. She was happily married and had a daughter and a son. The patient had less positive things to say about his younger sister, whom he described as needy and miserable. Next to his insistence that his grandmother was psychotic, his most negative description was reserved for his father, who died two years before our first analytic meeting. The father had sustained a heart attack sixteen years earlier (when the patient was ten) and had taken poor care of himself since, all the while relentlessly intimidating the family with his illness and possible death. The patient was extremely angry when discussing his father and commented that he had "not yet buried him."

Jan initially described his mother as sweet, passive, and dependent on her own mother, who had died shortly before the patient's father. This description of mother did not hold up in the analysis; Jan reported every conversation with her in exasperated and frustrated words and tones. She had been ill for several years and could speak only about herself and her suffering. There were few visits between the two, but they spoke on the telephone regularly. The patient did not see his mother as being much different from the person she had been during his childhood, except that although his hateful grandmother was no longer in the way, something else was. On the few occasions when he and his mother seemed close, it was because Jan was in the position of mothering her. As the analysis progressed, this relationship changed markedly, and he was able to create a situation in which his mother became more of a parent and even a friend.

The analysis proceeded with relative ease. After a great deal of shame and embarrassment accompanying the exposure of his sexual activities, Jan settled into a clear and intense father transference in which idealization played an important part. His relationships with others were passive and masochistic, and he complained bitterly of mistreatment by friends and colleagues. In the analysis he showed a deepening idealization of me and a quick change to incredible rage and subsequent sexualization at my failings and supposed lack of concern. Missed appointments and weekend breaks usually resulted in homosexual acting out.

Over time, three phases of the patient's relationship to the father were delineated. The first was a periodic disruption of the relationship. This was most clearly related to the sexualization, which represented an attempt to harness severe excitement (Goldberg 1975). Initially, a rather common occurrence, the sexualization gradually diminished in analysis. When Jan was able to give up his daily, ritualized masturbation, he recalled for the first time an important experience that centered around the father's working nights and coming home in time to have breakfast with his son. When the father was late, Jan would be unable to wait because he would have to leave for school. At these times he would carefully watch the minute hand of the clock and would almost be in pain as the last minute ticked away and he was forced to miss seeing his father. Often the father would bring home sweet rolls for breakfast, and on occasion, he would bring a special pastry that only his son liked. Jan remembered yearning for the special relationship with his father that that sweet roll represented. He also remembered that for some reason he could never ask his father to buy that special treat for him. In the analysis this was seen as the wish to merge or connect by having the analyst recognize the need without the patient's asking.

The second form of the relationship with the father was one of harmony. These recollections connected to the increasingly long periods of equilibrium in the analysis. The patient recalled joining his father on his many expeditions to sell his wares, an extra business activity for the father, who wanted to be more than a mere factory worker. Some of the factors contributing to the patient's not fitting in are evident in the father's lack of contentment with his own lot in life. In the analysis this was the period of the disappearance of sexualization.

The third relationship to the father was the most frightening one for Jan and had to do with the lost or absent father. This issue was always in the air in the analysis and was most likely to emerge during long vacations. The patient described his feeling about this as a feeling of falling apart and related it to both his father's heart attack and his death. Jan also recalled long periods of waiting quietly outside his father's door while he slept. He yearned for his father to awaken but feared his wrath if any noise woke him prematurely. This figure was the totally lost and then hated father. All these feelings were reexperienced and repeatedly interpreted in the analysis. After working through his paternal relationship, the analysis turned to the more frustrating one with the neglectful mother.

It may be of interest to try to explain why this man failed to gain a positive response from his mother. The interference offered by the grandmother was only one factor. Later I learned that his maternal grandfather was also an unusual person and perhaps even something of a misfit. He stayed away from the rest of the family, did carpentry work in a private area of his house, and never seemed to be upset by the rantings of his wife. The grandmother was best seen as delusional; her accusations against the grandfather were characteristic of jealousy and sexual betrayal. It is small wonder that the patient's mother behaved apprehensively toward her father. She may have had a parallel transference toward her own son, considering him strange, unusual, and frightening. It would be too superficial an explanation, however, to say that Jan identified with the grandfather as a misfit and lived out maternal expectations. There is little doubt that eccentricity can serve to organize a personality, but such postures or "identities" are always social phenomena that require in-depth psychological explanation. In this case, I concluded that the explanation lay in the fact that Jan was not properly mirrored by his mother, who could not free herself sufficiently from her own neurotic entanglements to do so adequately. When, of necessity, the patient turned from her to his father, seeking an avenue for self-expression and development, he also experienced failure, and here is where the analytic work was concentrated.

Coexisting with the analytic work relating to the idealizing and disappointing relationship with the father was the patient's ever-present fear that the analysis and the analyst were forcing him toward heterosexuality. He experienced marked improvement in every other area of life and repeatedly faced his fear and revulsion at being heterosexual. Although he had several women friends, he never had any intimate physical contact with them, and he could not manage much more than an occasional kiss. He could embrace neither his homosexuality nor the prospect of heterosexuality.

For Jan, all sex was disgusting; he hated his body and felt ugly and awkward. As the material in the analysis shifted and revealed his secret pleasure in his own specialness, he recalled how his aunt and sister had dressed him as a girl when he was quite young. His mother made fun of the small size of his penis and laughed at him whenever he was nude. Later, everyone seemed to laugh at the possibility of his dating. He spoke about a fantasy in which he announced his marriage. His family would be shocked. They thought of him as an eccentric, a "weirdo." Jan would have especially liked to tell his best friend's mother, who had only contempt for him and would have been crushed at his happiness. The analysis shifted to an intense feeling of hate toward those who could have responded positively to his achievements, his body, and his masculinity but failed to do so.

In summary, Jan turned primarily to his father for fulfillment of both mirroring and idealizing needs. Although he seemed less traumatized in the idealizing aspect of his personality, he showed the dual problems characteristic of most perverse disorders. What was so telling about this patient's problems was his inability to reconcile these two sectors of his personality. His grandiose, narcissistic self was not responded to by his preoccupied or threatened parents. His need for an idealizing relationship was equally frustrated. As one sector was repaired and reorganized, the other came more clearly into conflict with the environment and his selfobjects. A total solution to his problem would lie in the analysis of the unresolved grandiose fantasy, which carried the seed of a masculine self that needed responsiveness to grow. At every point in the transference, the developmental problem of fitting in came sharply into view. Neither a comfortable regression nor an easy road of progress was available to this man, who had not achieved a happy union with his selfobjects.

In rethinking this case, I have tried to come to grips with the patient's essential wish to be asexual. I think that this particular rehabilitation of his idealizing pole did indeed eliminate the sexualizations in his life. Nonetheless, he seemed unable to proceed with a happy heterosexuality or homosexuality. There was, in this case, an opportunity to examine some of the severe defects in the grandiose pole, but here too there was no chance for a heterosexual life. One can readily argue that the analysis was incomplete. Yet, although a nonsexual life may not be a satisfactory conclusion for most analysts, this man seems to be content and productive at this point, according to a rather long follow-up. What is suggested here is that the essentially intact homosexual pole of the self compensates for fragility and defect in the grandiose pole, but it does so without much sexual activity. After sexualization is removed, the self may pursue other activities that can be seen as sublimated, neutralized, or autonomous. What sexual activity is available for him is homosexual, but that seems not to be a major part of his life. I nevertheless claim that his compensatory structure is homosexual on the basis of his fantasies and sense of self, as well as his severely limited sexual life.

Case Three

My third case is of Michael, discussed earlier, and runs the risk of the critical assessment of incompleteness. It differs from the other two in that the predominant transference was that of the patient's exhibitionism. He entered his analysis with a clear wish not to be altered in his sexual orientation and, in fact, was reassured to that effect by his first analyst, who promised not to disturb it in any way. Although he did show evidence of sexualization in the transference, it was often in the service of handling a disruption in the pole of ambitions and grandiosity, and he managed to establish a significant homosexual relationship during his treatment. This sexual behavior seemed to be employed not so much for managing the potential loss of the selfobject, but more for a genuine form of involvement. That his major sexual orientation seemed derived to compensate for earlier defects did seem to be demonstrated by the severely defective aspects of this pole of grandiosity that emerged in the transference. The manifestations of this were his initial image of himself as sickly and defective. He benefited mightily from his analysis, but, as he had predicted, his sexuality was untouched, save to become less frantic and more comfortable. After he felt a long period of relative ease, he quit analysis. If he had been heterosexual, there is no doubt that he could be a fine presentation of a successful analysis. Seen as a rehabilitated self with a compensatory structure of homosexuality, he can still be considered analyzed. I will discuss reconsideration of the end point of analysis more fully in chapter 10.

Thus these three cases include a man who had no wish whatsoever to be other than homosexual (case 3), one who would have liked to be heterosexual (case 1), and one for whom all sex was distasteful, but homosexuality was tolerable (case 2). Case 3 had clearly used the idealizing pole to compensate for his problem of mirroring, but it had not done so adequately. His treatment, involving hypochondriacal and psychosomatic problems, was successful without much involvement of homosexuality. For case 1, his sexualization was evidence of a breakdown of his idealizing pole, and his analysis was also successful in rehabilitating that pole but with little attention paid to the grandiose pole. He therefore terminated with a better-functioning compensatory structure as a homosexual. Case 2 also focused mainly on idealization, but his analysis ended with the functioning compensatory structure of a homosexual with little sexual interest. Describing these cases in this manner may help to illustrate that the idealizing pole in some male homosexuals can become an adequately functioning compensatory structure and that the treatment of such individuals must be directed and controlled with that end-point configuration in mind. The compensatory pole is a more or less stable structure that serves the total self while it likewise handles the underlying structural defect.

Discussion

These three cases also illustrate the sequence of the origin of the compensatory structure of homosexuality. It is not my intention to explain all incidences of homosexual behavior by this thesis.

In some cases of male homosexuality it seems that early problems in development with the mirroring selfobject—that is the parental responsiveness to the masculine presentation—lead to a pursuit of the idealized selfobject for a structure of compensation. This configuration may itself be defective, and that deficiency may be handled, or defended, by sexualization. In some cases the sexualization may be of minimal significance, and a sexual solution involving a homosexual choice is adequate and gratifying. In other cases, the analysis serves primarily to work out the problems of sexualization. What results from this analytic resolution is not easy to predict. In the first case, the analysis fairly effectively eliminated the sexualization and yielded a man who wished to be heterosexual but probably could not be. The second case was someone who could not happily become either heterosexual or homosexual. Once the sexualization was eliminated and the ideal pole was rehabilitated, there seemed to be no ready or shame-free adoption of a sexual role. We should here think long and hard about asexuality as a possible self-configuration. The third case illustrates a compensatory structure that itself entered little into the analysis. This patient feared that the loss of the structure, which was organized around homosexuality, was a potential danger, so he allowed access only to the damaged pole of his self. Thus he made it clear that his treatment was to be directed to a self-defect in need of repair and not to one that seemed to be effectively compensatory for him.

It is all too easy to claim that these are cases of psychotherapy, incomplete analyses, or some other variant of an attempted or failed healing process. There is little doubt that there was significant improvement in these cases, but that is not the issue because they are offered not as evidence of effective treatment, but rather as examples of one type of problem that underlies homosexuality. It is the issue of the possible psychopathology of the male homosexual that draws our attention here.

Homosexuality needs a psychoanalytic psychology, whether

or not it is innate, genetic, or biologic. To abrogate this instrument of inquiry by pleading the relevance of biology is to agree implicitly that we are waiting for the triumph of the physical over the mental. Such a path is much too similar to other arbitrary divisions, such as considering food solely on the basis of caloric content rather than taste, or dismissing a book because the print is too small. These are different issues. Homosexuality needs a psychology, and it also needs a psychopathology, since it is often, but not always, in the service of a disordered development.

Homosexuality, however, does not need to be dismissed, disregarded, or given a position of special pleading. To claim it does not exist, as Stoller (1991) does, is to diminish us as clinicians who know of its presence and its possible problems. To insist that only homosexual therapists should treat such patients is to confuse familiarity with expertise and to exchange objectivity for a friendly disposition. And to fall back on the biological is to avoid the study altogether by a sleight of hand. It is equally without merit to evaluate homosexuality on the basis of its ego-syntonicity or ego-dystonicity. The first patient described is an example of someone who felt his sexual behavior to be at odds with his wishes but was unable to do much about it. If there is a fundamental structural deficit, it is a superficial exercise to posit a diagnosis based on something so socially determined as whether it is ego-dystonic. There is truth in the acceptance of one's homosexuality, but it may be in the awareness of the effectiveness of its serving as a compensatory structure.

If we reappraise homosexuality in terms of its self-organization, then we are obliged to clarify the status and nature of the selfobjects. For one thing, are they oedipal or preoedipal selfobjects? To return to the definition offered by the APA, it is clear that the dynamics described have to do with the oedipal phase. The emphasis is on a negative oedipal solution, with the little boy identifying with his mother and being sexually excited by men. Isay (1989) has suggested a variant of this in which the little boy is attracted to the father, who cannot tolerate his son's seductive or affectionate attitude. As oedipal selfobjects, either the mother or the father may fail to mirror positively the boy's burgeoning masculinity or seductiveness; a special case of this based on a biological propensity might well satisfy the Isay description. The important note of difference has to do with self-development, so that the mirroring selfobject conforms to and solidifies one's feeling about oneself. If the boy is not responded to by the mother or the father, he may disavow his masculinity and pursue the path of maintaining his self-esteem by idealizing selfobjects. The oedipal phase allows this turn to take on a sexual connotation, and the idealized selfobject may be a participant in this resolution. We should be wary, however, of limiting the study to this oedipal phase, although there may be a subgroup of unknown size of homosexuals who do qualify. Kohut (1984) emphasized that the oedipal complex does indeed follow faulty oedipal selfobject responses in the oedipal phase. In most cases evidence exists of earlier selfobject failures that may indeed get caught up in either the sexuality of the oedipal period or in nonsexual behavior disorders. It is once again in the unfolding of the transference that we see evidence of early preoedipal self-object failures, most particularly in the sphere of reality testing. Just as Glover (1932) and later Chasseguet-Smirgel (1991) noted, there is often a defective sense of reality in perversion. I think one may differentiate sexual disorders along the axis of reality (Gedo and Goldberg 1971). (Of course this may also be true of heterosexuality.) Regardless of the manifest content, it is most unusual not to see faulty reality testing accompanying the sexualization of perverse activity, and it was readily apparent in at least one of the cases described above. There are, however, other cases where there is no indication of such a split, where there is little or no negative affect associated with the sexual behavior, and where the reintegrated self functions smoothly as homosexual.

Conclusions

In some patients who satisfy in whole or in part the four behavioral components of homosexuality delineated by Friedman (1988), a particular selfobject transference develops in psychoanalysis. This transference configuration is an idealizing one, and it is often the site of various levels of sexualization. The sexualization of the transference usually subsides after a period of stability, and the major work of analysis is to rehabilitate this sector or pole of the self. What emerges is a more or less stable selfobject configuration that assumes the status of a compensatory structure. Profound defects in the grandiose pole of the self are readily apparent, but it is usually not possible to engage this pole in the analysis. If, as illustrated in one of the cases, there appears to be some therapeutic work in this area, the resultant self-configuration remains primarily that of an idealized pole that serves as a compensatory structure and thereupon severely limits a full analytic experience with the pole of ambitions and exhibitionism. Therefore, the resultant self is a form of idealization serving to maintain self-cohesion and self-esteem. This self can then participate in sexual activity with a homosexual object choice without undue vulnerability to the self, but it may also on occasion yield a relatively asexual individual.

Although one may posit an oedipal resolution with a homosexual object choice, often earlier selfobject difficulties and self-defects, particularly in the grandiose, exhibitionistic pole, become apparent in treatment, along with a defect of idealization. The major evidence of this duality of defects is in the area of reality and reality testing. This corresponds to a similar problem seen in many other forms of perversion. That homosexual behavior is a possible result of genetic and biologic factors does not mean that it is not a proper subject for a depth-psychological study, and the thesis presented here underscores its place in the perspective of self psychology.

I turn next to a study of heterosexual behavior that qualifies as perverse, that is, it involves sexualization because of a structural fragility. The behavior is pathological but only when we determine the underlying structure do we see why.

7
Sexualization, the Depleted Self, and Lovesickness

The experience of sexual excitement, like all intense emotions, can serve more than one purpose, have more than a single meaning, and so can be enlisted in a range of normal to abnormal psychological configurations. The sexualizations employed to bolster a fragile self-structure are, of course, usually pleasurable in and of themselves, but they can be further deployed in numerous defensive maneuvers (such as disavowal) that either share the aim of maintaining self-cohesion or independently guard the self against further pain and discomfort. Thus the pleasure of sexual excitement may carry with it a burden: the task of relieving a more profound disturbance of the self. At times the supposed pleasure seeking assumes a quality of frantic hyperactivity, as the excitement itself takes a secondary role to relief of the underlying discomfort, which is more often than not experienced as a hollowness or empty sense of depression. The effort here seems to be less in the direction of stopping a regression that is the hallmark of sexualization and more toward inducing a feeling of vitality in the self. One rather exaggerated form of a self in search of feeling alive is the syndrome of erotomania, or lovesickness: the overwhelming and usually sudden head-over-heels falling in love that is intense, all-consuming, and often, unfortunately, inappropriate. It is easily seen as something approaching the sort of blindness I described in discussing splitting. It may on occasion become an answer to a profound and painful depressive state. Such a state is quickly layered over by a peculiar form of sexual excitement associated with the almost desperate feeling of being love-struck. I suggest that this symptom is a prototype of certain forms of sexually maladaptive behavior used as defensive measures to handle more severe self-disturbances.

Before pursuing a clinical discussion, it is necessary to position the central role of sexual excitation as the remedy for a depleted self. The usual consideration of depression is routinely divided by psychoanalytic self psychology into those forms involving guilt—that is, superego injunctions—versus those that describe a hollowness and sadness with no evidence of wrongdoing or punitive fantasies. The latter form of depression is felt to be due to depletion or to the essential unresponsiveness of one's selfobjects. In fact, Kohut (1977) at one point divided the pathology of the self into those disorders involving fragmentation and those encompassing depletion (p. 243). The second group was centered on a world of unmirrored ambitions, devoid of ideals. On the basis of this division, there seemed to be a possibility of constructing a better classification of self psychopathology, one that goes beyond a single, rather large and amorphous group of selfobject failures. Indeed, the popular claim that in demanding compliance from a child parents do not allow for the child's independent development (Brandchaft 1993)—that is, a failed selfobject responsiveness occurs—is one example of this large, poorly differentiated group. That group requires that the compliant child who succeeds in forming self-cohesion be differentiated from the child who fails in this developmental task. Each child may be asked by the parent for one type of behavior rather than another—given one parental interpretation of reality rather than another—but nowhere is it clear that one interpretation leads to pathology and another to an acceptable social conformity. The concept of selfobject failure, correct as it may be, is not a focused enough explanation to allow us to expect one result rather than another. Clearly, there is much more that must be said about the particulars of parental responsiveness before a better classification is available to us. For now, there are two fundamental forms: the self of fragmentation and the enfeebled self. It is the second that uses sexual excitation as a vitalizing and strengthening action of ameliorization—that is, the use of sex to feel alive. Such a use of sexualization is to be differentiated from the active effort to stem regression or to fill in a missing structural defect, a usage aimed at healing impending fragmentation.

The self of hollowness or depletion is often confronted in treatment only after the particular layer of behavioral efforts to overcome it is analyzed and put to one side. We are then able to observe a person who is radically different from his or her initial presentation, one often superficially characterized by a plethora of frantic activity. Though it is never warranted to apply this generalization to a diagnostic category, my experience with these cases is that lifting the hyperactivity reveals not only depression but a widespread emotional and intellectual shallowness as well. The cases I offer as representative were not only strikingly uninvolved with other people in general but also fundamentally uninteresting as individuals. They could easily be considered persons lacking inner resources in the ordinary sense of being thoroughly limited; they had little involvement in depth in much of anything. In fact, they were quick to complain that nothing much mattered to them and that they had little enthusiasm for anything. Rather surprisingly, being alone was such a rare event that they neither especially dreaded it nor desired it, even though it would be a stark display of the empty life they experienced. This fact is significant in that the times of solitude were avoided so successfully that the emptiness was not a presenting symptom but was only later fully evoked in treatment. These patients in some small measure had therefore either succeeded in covering their emptiness with hyperactivity or had in an equally substantive fashion experienced life as burdensome because of the many unrewarding but time-consuming duties demanded of them. Thus, they moved from highs to lows with a characteristic shallowness at each extreme. I make no attempt to examine the varied subjective phenomena enlisted in the description of these states, since some distinguish emptiness from boredom (Meares 1993) while others claim that a false self hides the essence of the patient's true self (Winnicott 1960). Rather, I merely want to explicate the place of sexual excitation in the effort to avoid the experience of hollowness. I move now to the clinical phenomenon of lovesickness.

Clinical Illustrations: Lovesickness and Self-Depletion

Being sick with love in some way touches us all. Though many may claim to have escaped it, we are surrounded by examples of the malady in poetry, novels, movies, and song. True and lasting lovesickness is never simply a flirtation with the virus. Rather, it is an all-consuming, painful, and oppressive feeling that possesses its victims and makes them marionettes to the puppeteer, Eros. It ranges from the mildest form of short-lived infatuation, or puppy love, to the erotomania described by Emil Kraepelin and Gatian de Clerambault (Segal 1989), a syndrome marked by the systematized delusion of passionate love for another person. Points on the spectrum are often characterized as illnesses (being "sick with love"), and of late an end point has become a bona fide member of the psychiatric book of illnesses (the DSM-III-R), where it joins a group of delusional (paranoid) disorders. Here it qualifies perhaps as an extreme example in the continuum of lovesickness. That it is an illness that cannot be ignored or tolerated is clear, inasmuch as it usually subordinates the conduct of ordinary life to its demands. What is interesting and perhaps most peculiar, there is no agreement as to its treatment or cure, although there is a surprising consensus that one either overcomes it or submits to it, otherwise it magically goes away by itself. What to do until that resolution comes about is a matter for folklore, which encompasses an extraordinary number of experts and advice. Yet the most surprising contrast to the abundance of cures is the single voice of the victims: there is but one cure to lovesickness and it is love. They are all convinced of that.

Psychiatric and Psychoanalytic Literature

The focus of this brief review is on the particular disorders of love characterized by the symptom of erotomania, the delusional belief that one is passionately loved by another. A recent revisiting of this symptom by psychiatric investigators has prompted a new concern for its status in terms of diagnosis and clinical course. Whereas some see it as a singular delusion in its own right (Rudden, Sweeney, and Francis 1990, 625), some claim that it is related to paranoia, others link it to schizophrenia, and some to affective disorders. The claim that it is more prevalent in women is disputed, but usually there is felt to be about a 75 percent female predominance. The various opinions may point to the need for a better ordering of narcissistic behavior disorders. In men there seems to be a variation in which the man is in the grips of an intense attachment to an unrequited love. Though there is debate about what is the best term for this variation of the symptom—from obsessive love to nondelusional erotomania—there is agreement that the malady itself is rather widespread.

There is likewise a range of opinion as to the clinical course and optimal treatment for the symptom or symptom complex. The general view is that it is most refractory to treatment, but this is somewhat tempered by reports of a subgroup of patients who are said to have a better clinical course with fewer hospitalizations (Rudden, Sweeney, and Francis, 627). Treatment is said to range from lithium to what can only be called unspecified intervention (p. 626) since no details are given as to exactly what is done to or with the patients. The missing component in the psychiatric literature is that of a psychological explanation for erotomania.

Freud's variations on the theme of "I love him" (1911), elaborated on in the Schreber case, were used to explain erotomania following the formula "I do not love him, I love her, because she loves me." The intense attachment of a man to a woman is but a version of the formula, and, although it was still felt to stem from the male patient's homosexual longings, there seems no need to separate the delusion of being loved from that of demanding another's love, save for the step that brings one close to psychosis. In fact, as Otto Fenichel (1945, 432) says, a man who projects his exaggerated desire for an object onto a woman is truly "persecuted with love."

The psychoanalytic literature on lovesickness is surprisingly sparse. It is as though love remains outside psychopathology, perhaps because no one complains of it unless and until it becomes a sickness. One exception is Kernberg (1974), who presents a developmental schema for being able to fall in love as well as a description of the characteristics of mature love. The ability to fall in love, he says, is based on the full development of oral and body-surface erotism and its integration into total object relations. In this he echoes D. W. Winnicott's prerequisite for the development of the capacity for concern for another. Kernberg describes mature love as consisting of the capacity to fall in love, to be tender, to have a sophisticated idealization, and to identify and empathize with the love object. The consecutive stages of development of internalized object relations supply the foundation for this descriptive, clinical assessment. Kernberg's own review of the literature reflects the paucity of contributions by psychoanalysts to the subject, but one is well served by the works of Robert Bak (1973), Martin Bergmann (1971), and Irene Josselyn (1971), all of whom connect the capacity to love to the ability to experience depression and to mourn. Mature love lies on a developmental line directed toward achieving that capacity.

Loving is therefore a capacity, an achievement, and a mark of growth and maturity. Narcissistic, borderline, and primitive patients may have sexual relations, idealized relations, and even stable relations, but they do not have "true love." Michael Balint (1948) says that love includes idealization, tenderness, and a special form of identification. Fenichel (1945) tells us that one can speak of love only when one's own satisfaction cannot be achieved without satisfying the object as well (p. 84). On the whole, although the true nature of love may elude psychoanalysis, there is no lack of authoritative statements about the psychopathology of love.

Persons who need to feel love but cannot love actively are considered to be "love addicts" (Fenichel, 387). They are described as inconsiderate people who demand that others understand their feelings. The origin of this "archaic type of self-esteem regulation" (p. 388) is said to be the wish to regain the feeling of infantile omnipotence by projecting it onto parents and thereupon participate in parental omnipotence. Such participation is said to be the feeling of being loved. If one is overly narcissistic, the need for self-love overshadows the love for the other. A higher, postnarcissistic love occurs with the capacity for object love, and thus a new self-respect emerges (p. 85). We must study narcissism in order to understand lovesickness better.

Victor Tausk (1933) discussed the early stages of narcissism as characterized by absolute self-satisfaction without others and without a world. He felt that this innate narcissism was followed by a pathological feeling of estrangement and then a projection of this discomfort onto the outer world. A subsequent sense of persecution may be formed by the construction of an influencing machine (the classical symbol of Tausk), which is a summation of some or all of the pathology projected outward. This machine represents a projection of the entire body. It controls, regulates, and may exploit the person. Kohut (1972) elaborated this scheme by considering the machine an early, if pathological, phase in the development of the idealized parental imago, a stage in a developmental line of narcissism. For most analytic writers, lovesickness is a pathological condition related to early difficulties in the deployment of narcissistic concerns. Whether one believes that true love goes beyond narcissism or is a manifestation of more mature narcissism, there seems to be a consensus that archaic or primitive narcissism is responsible for the difficulties in love ranging from being possessed by love in erotomania to the excessive idealization that accompanies ordinary love.

Freud (1922) felt that being in love consisted in a flowing over of libido onto the object and that in many forms of love-choice the object serves as a substitute for some unattained ideal: "We love it on account of the perfections which we have striven to reach for our own ego, and which we should now like to procure in this roundabout way as a means of satisfaction of our narcissism" (pp. 112–13). Thus we love both to fulfill ourselves and to heal ourselves. It seems that we use love as a balm and a cure, even if it is not that elusive "true" state.

The sequence of perfect self-love followed by pain or discomfort that is projected outward is then resolved in the form of the sought-for love object, which is seen as a source of peace and pleasure. This object can be persecutory as well, but, at heart, the longed-for object is always a bit of the long-lost perfection of the self. Thus it is always narcissistic, and its attainment leads to perfect bliss. It need have no special properties of its own since it fundamentally *is* the self. For Tausk, it was often a representation of the genitals, and the hurtful machines that he wrote about were embodiments of genital irritation. The particular ingredients of the initial pain and the subsequent cure vary over a wide range of incidents and persons, but the basic ingredient is narcissistic injury, and the basic cure is a balm to the self.

In presenting the clinical material that follows I aim to show a range of the pathology of lovesickness as well as a range of therapy. The treatment covers both psychotherapy and psychoanalysis and demonstrates an earlier thesis (Goldberg 1981) that points out the distinction between the two. The first case demonstrates the treatment of lovesickness, which involves the repair of the injured self and the emergence of the underlying depression. The second case is of a patient in analysis who also revealed an empty depression. Though these two patients may share a common symptom, it is not my intent to compare them in terms of diagnosis or course of treatment. My point is that love-sickness serves primarily to vitalize a depleted state of the self.

Clinical Case 1

"Henry" is a professional man in his late twenties who went to see a psychiatrist because he was hopelessly in love with a woman who cared little for him but whose psychic presence dominated almost every moment of his waking life. He told me that he was agitated and upset and thought he could feel better only once he had obtained the love of this woman. She was difficult for me to imagine, since the patient had little to say about her; he had seen her only a few times and had never been on intimate terms with her. He insisted that she satisfied all his "specs" for a woman—a list devoted primarily to physical attributes. He wanted only to talk about her and figure her out, to gain advice and reassurance about how to have her. There was but a secondary recognition that perhaps his supposed love was exaggerated and unreal. At no time, however, did he or could he conceal his intense psychological pain, which was an incessant yearning.

Henry had little to say about his past except that such sweeping states of love had overcome him on previous occasions. Though he insisted that this time was different and special, he felt he was especially prone to falling in love with the sort of woman who was physically appealing and about whom he knew little. This latest episode was connected in time to the death of his father. He said he could not be sure if he was depressed because of grief over that loss or because of his unrequited love. Yet he talked incessantly about his longed-for love and had little to say about his lost parent.

Henry came for treatment on the advice of friends but admitted that he had seen other therapists, both while in college and more recently, and had shopped around for the right person. I felt pleased at winning the lottery. As the treatment—a twice-per-week, face-to-face arrangement—proceeded, however, I found him terribly boring and frustrating. I never seemed to know what was happening in his life, which seemed shallow and empty, though he mentioned many people as passing through. His love dominated everything. The unloved lover occasionally talked to his paramour on the telephone, but she was cool and careful not to give him any hope or encouragement. He wanted only to marry, and he made elaborate plans for their future together. At times I thought that his intense passion was so close to a delusion that I feared he could never be disabused of it. He compared himself to John Hinckley and Hinckley's yearning for Jodie Foster, but he immediately insisted that he was different because he felt he really knew this person and his love was genuine. One day he managed to meet and talk to someone who had dated the woman and next told me of a dream: He was flying and being chased by helicopters. He was frightened but suddenly managed to be free of them and to "soar." He felt wonderful in the dream, convinced that he was every bit as good as this other man who had dated his love and that he would be able to succeed in winning her.

Such moments of pleasure were rare; he was usually miserable. The phone was his only contact with the woman, and he had come to fear it and then become captured by it. Finally, he managed to get his beloved to agree to see him and decided to propose. I listened in amazement as he told me of an elaborate arrangement involving dinner, music, a proposal, and the presentation of a ring. I tried gently to tell him that this was really a first date, even though he might feel it to be a fulfillment of his life's dream. My wish to be a calm and rational presence was probably betrayed by the absolute dumbfoundedness that accompanied my comments, but my amazement intensified as he agreed with me. Once again I felt that there was a part of him that was sane and tied to reality, a part that sat and watched the incredible scene unfold. My therapeutic tactic was a simple one; I asked him to tell me what actually went on in his life so that I could connect these real events with his fantastic flight to dreams of his loved one.

The couple kept their date. They did not seem to have a good time, and the woman turned out not to be a very nice person. Nevertheless, my patient's love continued unabated. He told me of a dream of oral sex in which tentacles of her vagina extended to entangle and capture him, and he was in a state of bliss. I was disheartened.

He continued his hot pursuit of this woman until she clearly told him that there was no future for them. She said to him: "You've made me up." He was devastated and talked of suicide. He resolved not to see her (an easy resolution and one he made frequently since he never succeeded in managing another date anyway) or call her. For a short while he said he felt better and described a lifting of his depression—but not for long. During the interlude, however, he managed to tell me a little of his early life: one dominated by a stern and demanding father and a compliant and pleasing mother. Father was a perfectionist. He came home every night to a dinner painstakingly prepared by mother, who was inevitably crestfallen as her husband managed to discover some flaw and become angry. The patient joined in the effort to please this irascible man and felt that he rarely succeeded.

He saw himself as someone who tries hard to be perfect. His fondest pursuit was mechanical drawing, a labor that led to absolutely perfect constructions. He had no difficulty at all in claiming that his longed-for love was the true embodiment of perfection and that their union would capture that elusive state in a permanent form for him.

As he spoke more of his father there were many positive memories as well as negative ones, although memories of his mother were more elusive and vague. As the treatment proceeded, he clearly charged me with the task of being the perfect person: one who would "magically" cure him. His reference to a magical cure was not simply a figure of speech; he was unhesitating in asking me to say something that would make him better, to "figure it out" so that he could once again be happy. Yet his past life revealed little enduring happiness, evidenced by his remembering that he occasionally thought of suicide in high school and suffered periodic depression. He reported a heavy use of marijuana in his teens and continuing occasional use of marijuana, cocaine, angel dust, and other substances. His medication was rarely successful, and he counted more and more on therapy.

After about six months of treatment the patient was able to recount a coherent story of his activities, and we could pinpoint the turning of his mind to his beloved at distinct moments of loneliness, hurt feelings, and feelings of inadequacy. Only at those times was I lifted to a state of interested involvement, since much of the other portion of the therapy consisted of the patient's struggle to understand the woman he loved and of asking me whether I was paying attention and whether I could tell him that he would soon be better. I often shared his bewilderment and befuddlement.

He slowly got better. He began to stay away from the woman, to stop calling her or planning to be with her, and he had moments of relief. It is of interest that he described these periods of relief as equivalent to those rare moments when he felt he did, could, or would have her. Love here seemed to take the form of peace and contentment rather than ecstasy and fulfillment. It was more of a balm than a peak experience.

The treatment was to be limited to one year, and as the end of that period approached, the patient had to move to a new position in a different city. His condition worsened at the prospect of leaving, and he became more dependent and began to talk about suicide. As the delusional quality of his lost love dissipated, the inevitable confrontation with reality was overwhelming. He felt lost and empty. He was not up to the demands of his new job. He said that he learned nothing in his training and needed to begin again. I think of a child who has failed to fill in the details of growing up with an idealizable parent and who therefore has to gulp it all down in one fell swoop—a child lacking in essential psychological structure. Leaving his therapy was more than the patient could handle, and during a visit home, he was hospitalized for a week. He spoke to me on the phone, was soon discharged, and returned to treatment. He decided to move on to the new city and sounded reasonable and less depressed, although he claimed to be anxious every morning on awakening. We saw each other until he left. He discontinued the medication given to him in the hospital with no difficulty. He called me from the new place, sounding as good as he had been; he decided to continue treatment with someone there. I felt less worried about him and began to think that at least his lovesickness was cured. Over the years he has sometimes called. He has remained in a state of depression with no return of the erotomania. He is realistic and empty.

Clinical Case 2

This patient is a forty-two-year-old professional man who has been married for five years but has been a Don Juan for much of his life. "George" said he was fairly happy with his wife, whom he described as the only woman he had ever met of whom he did not tire. However, he continually considerd divorce because of their failure to have children, coupled with his feeling that life would be incomplete without a child. Marriage and occasional sexual escapades were not the whole of George's love life, which had been punctuated by episodes of extreme and overwhelming love for certain women. He said that this sort of love was in no way similar to what he had for his wife or his other bed partners but rather was an all-consuming preoccupation with the women with whom he fell in love, usually without knowing them at all. He became totally devoted to the pursuit of the woman, and this occupied all his waking hours. He was sick with love and was relieved only when he could spend time with his beloved. This head-over-heels falling in love had occurred periodically since his adolescence and was the immediate cause for his seeking psychoanalysis. He had two or three previous psychotherapies but said they amounted to little more than support. His uncertainty about the number of therapies was based on a statement he recalled from his first course of treatment: the therapist had said that he thought George was a pleasant person but that he did not know him at all. The most recent (and referring) therapist joined in this appraisal of George as an enigma. No one knows him, and his treatments do not amount to much.

The history of the patient is uneventful; he described himself as never being very interested or involved in anything. His mother was sweet and simple; his deceased father was someone he had been fond of but rarely had much to say to; his sister was a nice person who lived in another state and with whom he spoke about once a year. George was successful in his work, but it was a labor of superficial contacts and conclusions. He was quick to characterize himself as superficial; someone not interested in many things, including the women in his life—with the singular exception of his wife. For him, the occasional women who inhabited the world of overwhelming love were more objects of pain than of interest.

The women at the center of this man's lovesickness were usually striking but difficult people. He absolutely adored them and uniformly discovered that they were untrustworthy, inconsiderate, or downright cruel. He pursued them with a passion that does not spend itself, even when he discovered their obvious flaws. He often fell out of love just as quickly as he fell in love, but this reversal was usually after many months of heartache and disappointment, accompanied by a blindness to the failings of his paramour. The cessation of his lovesickness was not caused by a recognition of being mistreated; rather, it happened suddenly and inexplicably and was peculiarly complete and absolute. He cared not a whit for these women after his passion ended.

He said that he put these particular women on a pedestal and that—in his words—they "allowed" him to go to bed with them. By this he meant that the women cared, but he learned later (usually long after he had been manipulated and used) that this was not true. In the beginning much of this patient's treatment was devoted to a detailed accounting of his relations with the various "loves" of his life. His treatment, in fact, began when he was in the throes of a cycle of lovesickness and was advised by a therapist to undergo psychoanalysis. He followed this advice, began analysis, and soon after lost interest in the woman. Indeed, his analysis was characterized by the absence of lovesickness as well as by a steady diminution in philandering.

Another feature that dominated the early period of analysis with George was his justifiable claim of being a man of virtue. Although reportedly surrounded by colleagues who were unreliable, untrustworthy, and uncaring of their fellows, George insisted on living a life of honesty, integrity, and reliability. He was known as someone who never cheated or cared much about money, who always kept his word, who could be called on at any time to fulfill a task, and who consistently served as an ideal to younger men. Many of his early analytic hours were spent distancing himself from scoundrels of various kinds, and there was never a hint that this experience was anything but genuine. He confessed that he felt ridiculous in claiming high ideals while cheating on his wife with little or no compunction. Thus the patient clearly demonstrated and presented a disparity or split in the psychological arena of ideals and values.

The other striking phenomenon of this analysis was the gradual reappearance in dreams of the patient's father: a man who became a cardiac cripple when George was ten years old. As the father again became alive and real in analysis, George had a series of dreams about something being missing. (He dreamed, for example, of a hernia operation in which there was not enough tissue to cover the wound.) In the transference the dreams represented George's chronic inability to come for full sessions at all the appointed hours and in the associations his insistence that there was nothing deep to be discovered in him. I pursued the matter of the dreams as a defense against underlying painful issues. At first I felt that his conflicts lay beneath a defense of superficiality but soon found myself wondering whether George was truly empty. A telling example of the reality of his emptiness came when he considered the subject of "something missing." He said he had a strong emotional bond with his father but always felt that he did not get enough from him. Just what it was that he did not get focused primarily on George's knowing about and being interested in things. He felt he was just like his dad: he had no interests. His father was a gambler who played cards whenever he was not working—when he went on vacation, when he got home from work, and when he was ill with heart disease. Although the father sounded like a sad person to me, George told me he was more bored than sad. Father and son rarely spoke to one another, and once, when the son asked the father why he had stayed in what seemed to be an unhappy marriage, the father replied that sometimes it was better to put up with things. Though George also gambled on occasion, he hardly qualified as a pathological gambler, as his father did. Although he lacked interest in many things, he was rarely bored as much as he was restless and discontented. His chronicle of his life's activities was that of a busy person who did all the right things, was liked, appreciated, and even admired by colleagues and friends, was a reliable friend and family man, but who felt dissatisfied, empty, and unfulfilled. For him there were no real pleasures in life, save episodic sexual exploits and periodic longings for women with whom he fell in love. As analysis proceeded we came upon the empty depression that underlay these symptoms. George came to sessions more regularly and felt connected, all the while claiming that he had nothing to say. He confronted an intense feeling of running in place with a feeling of no real accomplishment or fulfillment. Falling in love was a quick fix and a sure cure. Psychoanalysis was a process of structural reorganization that allowed for filling in the missing aspects of the idealized selfobject: the father who was equally empty and hidden from view. The treatment turned when George began to have moments of enjoying being with people, diminished restlessness, and a modicum of enthusiasm. In a way, he began to connect more with the world.

Discussion

The particular dramatic form lovesickness takes, as well as its role in most of our lives in a milder form, may argue against including it in the family of perversions. Yet it is clearly a form of sexualization, is regularly accompanied by a vertical split that may be severe enough to qualify the patient as delusional, and seems just as clearly to be employed in the service of maintaining the self. The two cases I have presented reveal lovesickness as an effort to escape the pain of self-depletion only to enter the agony of unrequited love. The range of these forms of infatuation is broad enough to reveal that the determining factor in the disorder is not the particular dynamics of the individual patient, the existence of disavowal, or the presence of sexualization, but rather a combination of the three.

The minimum requirement for this state is a suspension of reality, and the two clinical cases clearly show the illusory quality of the patients' relations with women. That iota of unreality is probably a part of all love relations that are characterized by an overidealization of the loved one. It allows for the blissful feelings associated with being in love and so gives the self the feeling of aliveness yearned for by unlucky lovesick victims, who achieve it only fleetingly and at great expense. The crucial component of love is not meant to be the full story of that sought-for state; it is the element that supports the self and reveals the narcissistic quality of love relations. The urgency of the search for someone to love reflects the depth of one's despair at confronting the hollowness of the self. The shallowness of investment in others represents the paucity of such investments in childhood and so demonstrates the amount of reparative and rehabilitative work that lies ahead in the treatment of such individuals. These patients show the dual problem of mirroring failure and a lack of idealization, but the fundamental self pathology centers around emptiness and its particular pain.

I turn next to another issue that is part and parcel of perversion and that may also serve to handle the discomfort of the depleted self: anger and accompanying phenomena. A sense of depletion is experienced by some patients as a state to be avoided at any cost. Although the emptiness must be obliterated and sexualization, including supposedly normal heterosexual intercourse, may work, often other types of behavior are needed as well.

8
Dehumanization, Rage, and Aggression in Perversions

From sexual activity as a means to vitalize a depleted self, I turn to a powerful set of emotions that are regularly linked with sexual behavior in explaining perversions. These emotions fall in the general category of anger or aggression and are regularly seen in the sensual experience of sexuality, in action ranging from normal to aberrant. It is said that some anger is present in all sexual behavior, and I have noted Stoller's (1975) view that hostility is the basis of all perversions. Here I differentiate between the normal aggression of sexual behavior and the reactive rage of other sexual activity. The way the sexual object is treated is commonly felt to be a distinguishing feature of perversion; that is, contempt and disdain for the other are said to be characteristic of dehumanization. I begin with that.

Dehumanization

Dehumanization is a code word for a severely negative attitude toward and treatment of another human being. It is a code word because it may summon up a set of feelings without demanding a clear definition. In fact, it covers a wide span of negative appraisals and mistreatments that needs to be carefully differentiated. The continuum begins with an evaluation of something—say, a rock or a piece of wood—as having no human qualities whatsoever. It may be said unequivocally that whatever one does with the rock, it has no moral or ethical repercussions, because it is beyond humanity. However, once we imbue anything or anyone else with human qualities, we take a step toward recognition, understanding, and possibly empathy. Because we anthropomorphize many things, from cars to Coke machines to quarks, the action itself is not a reliable indication that we feel something is truly human or humanlike.

The animal kingdom is where we begin to empathize. Indeed, the discovery of endorphin-like substances in fish has led many fishers to reconsider the calm with which they pulled a hook out of a fish, thinking surely it felt no pain. Here is the point when the issue of dehumanization has meaning: that moment when we concern ourselves with another's pain or discomfort versus the time when we are unable or unwilling to care. Dehumanization, however, arises not only when we are seemingly oblivious to another's pain but when we become participants in its production. In fact, we accuse someone of dehumanization when he or she treats someone else "like a rock"—without feeling—or like a human but without caring. These situations are, in fact, totally different states. It is one thing not to register someone else's unhappy state, to fail to read someone else's humanity. It is quite another to debase or hurt someone else purposefully. One must differentiate between kicking the car and kicking the cat.

The dehumanization so often claimed to be an element of certain sexual perversions may at times be without an awareness of the other's feelings. It is much more likely, however, to involve a clear and intentional mistreatment that requires the participation of the other's feelings, though not in a caring way. Sadism, humiliation, activity, and even inactivity of any kind in the sexual partner demand a special form of human reactiveness and relations. It is necessary to have an empathic union with the sexual object in order to effect a reasonable conclusion to the sexual act. That this union may range from a relative deadness to playacting to excruciating forms of pain is not to say that it is dehumanization. Sadly, it is altogether too human. Maurice Lever (1993), in his biography of the Marquis de Sade, writes that Sade's pessimistic view of nature is embodied in what he called *isolism,*" meaning the inability of the individual to communicate with any other individual. Lever says that we are thus, according to Sade, unable either to rejoice in another's happiness or sympathize with those in pain. For Sade, isolism is equivalent to deadness and sadism is the way to connect.

These connections within the human sphere must always be part of some element of empathy, since there is no meaning or significance outside the realm of empathy. The simple umbrella term *dehumanization* leads to a loss of meaning. That particular meaning can be regained only by the empathic effort to grasp precisely what the sexual object does for, with, or to the sexual act and actor. This definition highlights the fact that empathy serves only to connect and communicate with another and not to achieve a feeling that is good, right, or correct. Treating someone like an insect is inhuman only when there is no feeling, and this is rarely the case in the sexual perversions.

Rage

The rage or anger that accompanies many sexual acts, from heterosexual union to the most outrageous sadistic behavior, probably always has some element of wishing to hurt and knowing what it is like to be hurt. Even the blind rage of the most severe attacker contains a design to cause pain at its core and is human in that regard. Kohut (1973) likens the reactive rage of narcissism to that of a child with hurt feelings as well as to the feelings of a neurologically damaged adult who cannot control a limb or find a word. At one end Kohut posits the anger that arises when one's grandiosity is damaged; the other comes from the loss of control and the ensuing feeling of helplessness that reflects the trauma of a break of the merger with the omnipotent selfobject. The rage that follows is not one of besting an opponent but rather one of

vengeance, of unremitting and relentless revenge against the offender as well as, at times, the offending part. The anger that
follows narcissistic injury is aimed at restoring a previously intact state; it is designed to revenge oneself upon the one who has
done the damage as well as to reconstitute one's self. Rage, however, can never live alone, since it inevitably includes another
person, a selfobject.

The therapist yawns. He tries mightily to hide or suppress it,
but it is astonishingly audible and visible. The patient, a woman,
pauses in her tale and instead launches a tirade against the hap-
less therapist, who is ashamed and yet unwilling at that moment
to be contrite. He feels that his yawn was involuntary and could
only be suppressed or disguised. The patient feels that it bespeaks the therapist's lack of interest in or downright boredom
with her, and this so increases her wrath that the yawn now
becomes the center of her remarks. As she berates her therapist
because of the damage done to her self-image and self-esteem, he
feels shame replaced by anger at this carping and uncooperative
patient. He wishes she would shut up and go back to the topic of
that long-vanished pre-yawn state. She feels that her agenda for
the day's work has been usurped by a callous therapist. Soon
both are angry, unyielding, and on the verge of hating one another. The crescendo of feelings that arises from a harmless
bodily act leads to a reciprocal state of alienation and anger that
locks both participants in a vise of implacable hostility.

Aggression versus Rage

Compare that initially innocent yawning scene and its attendant
reciprocal rage to the statement of Freud (1905) that the sexuality of most male human beings contains an element of aggres-
siveness, "a desire to subjugate" (p. 157) that is soon impercepti-
bly equated by some with destruction and rage. Perhaps the idea
of aggression as equated with destruction occurs too readily to

be accurate. Stoller (1975) quotes Hans Küng as saying that destructive impulses are typical of all forms of perversions (p. 106). Stoller goes on to explain that the erotic pleasure in sexuality, and especially in perversions, is the desire of a man, for example, to act forcefully upon an unwilling woman, to defeat her, to get revenge for past frustrations, to degrade her, and to triumph over her. He connects this essential core of hostility in all perversions to childhood defeats and frustrations, in which the child's biological demands were sadistically controlled by the parents. He concludes that the central issue in perversion is the struggle for control. Yet surely this is only one instigator of rage, and just as Freud moved aggression into destruction, this view seems to collapse it all into a single form.

Kohut (1973) says that narcissistic rage occurs when either the self or the other fails to live up to the expectations directed at their function, whether by the child who insists on his or her own grandiosity and omnipotence or by the adult who lives with these narcissistic structures unmodified. Intense and violent rage arises in those individuals for whom a sense of absolute control over an archaic environment is indispensable because the maintenance of self-esteem—as well as of the self per se—depends on the unconditional availability of an admiring self-object or the opportunity for a merger with an idealized one. The self of an offended person expects to exercise full control over those whose independence and other-ness is an offense (p. 386).

Some authors believe that the wish to subjugate (Freud 1905) soon leads to the wish to destroy and to hurt. Kohut, however, separates this primary aggression from rage. The rage reaction stems from a loss of control as well as from an injury to one's self-esteem, as in the yawning incident. There is the form that follows injury (the yawn) and another, which comes from a loss of control.

Here is an example of this second kind of rage. An analytic patient returns from the weekend separation for a single appointment before a two-week separation. He tells of intense homosexual voyeurism over the weekend with an almost unbearable need to look at men. He also reports a dream of a person who can communicate by satellite but has not gotten connected to it. He associates to his last appointment during and following which he was angry because his analyst had failed to analyze a dream adequately. The patient was fairly sure that his analyst was capable of explaining the dream's meaning but had desisted as part of a grand plan. In truth, the patient explained, he felt like a marionette under the control of the analyst. The analyst asked the patient whether he preferred that the analyst toy with him rather than be intellectually limited and thus show his inadequacy in interpreting the dream. The patient replied without hesitation that he absolutely wanted his analyst to know everything, even if it meant that material would be withheld from him. There was a comfort, he said, in knowing there was a plan and no pleasure at all in the analyst's being limited and inadequate. This patient's father had either been preoccupied or pathetic, but certainly the patient had no memory of his being either cruel or comforting.

We can reconstruct the patient's impending loss of the sustaining idealized selfobject. He reacts to the anticipated separation with a sexualization in the form of voyeurism, an activity that seems only vaguely to disguise his intense wish to see inside the psyche of the alienated and preoccupied father. The complaint about the analyst's withholding knowledge is a recognition by the patient of a failure in the relationship and a regression to the feeling of being abused and mistreated. As he recognizes his inability to control the analyst as a selfobject, he experiences the rage that comes from helplessness, from a self made to feel inadequate by the independence and separateness of the other. All of this repeats some essential moment of his childhood. The sexuality aims to hold on to and control the support of the selfobject. The hostility is a reaction to the analyst as selfobject and the selfobject's freedom to leave. The particular configuration of the selfobject is revealed by the fantasy that the analyst is omniscient as well as benevolent. The satellite in the dream may show the essentially narcissistic configuration of the analytic relation. The analyst is in complete control, and it is all for the patient's own good. There is, at this point, no room for the fallibility of the analyst and no place for the simple disillusionment we would hope for in normal development, which was clearly overly traumatic for this man, who remembers that in his childhood his father was weak or absent, both physically and emotionally.

The yawning therapist who injured the patient's grandiosity and the separating analyst who challenged the patient's absolute control each evoked a rage reaction in the patient. The two figures satisfy Kohut's criteria for narcissistic rage, which has the "specific psychological flavor" of a need for revenge to right a wrong and undo a hurt. Narcissistic rage is so common and familiar that it is clearly separate from other forms of aggression, which aim only for success and not for revenge. Only in selected cases do we see the close alliance of this rageful response and irresistible sexuality.

We see the regular and ordinary occurrence of rage in everyday situations from the inevitable slights of day-to-day living to the hurts of treatment. No one is free of hurt and anger, although the range and display of rage and the recovery from rage are enormous. In moving to the sexual sphere, however, we find a fairly representative literature (Kernberg 1991; Stoller 1975) claiming that some hostility or sadism is an expected and accepted part of all sexual activity and is not to be considered perverse or abnormal. It is an interesting exercise in vicarious introspection to tease out the nature of that supposedly normal wish to hurt. The question is whether it is a natural part of sexual expression, a remnant of the competitive feeling of sexual triumph, or even perhaps a bit of reactive rage that has echoes of a narcissistic fragility.

For some there is no doubt. Chasseguet-Smirgel (1991) tells of a patient transforming object relations into segments representing feces. This is said to be a destructive relationship with the analyst. Stoller (1975), as I have noted, stresses the hostile and aggressive aspect of perversion. Kernberg (1993) claims that his observations regarding borderlines correspond to those of perversions and include an excess of aggression in pregenital (particularly oral) and oedipal relations. Hate is one of the essences of perversion for these writers. It may be, however, that once aggression per se is put aside, rage becomes amenable to explanation.

Dehumanization and Disavowal

Let us return in the effort to include dehumanization in the discussion to the patient mentioned earlier whose sexual escapades consisted of visiting a nearby park, where anonymous men would perform fellatio on seemingly disembodied penises or on bodies with penises but without attached persons. This is probably an extreme example of dehumanization. The patient felt drawn to the site, felt no specific feelings during the act, save sexual excitement and pleasure, but thereafter experienced waves of disgust and shame. This type of perverse behavior represents the most common sequence of emotions in patients who seek treatment and is very much at odds with reports that characterize "an idealization of the specific perversion of the individual patient as vastly superior to 'ordinary' genital relations (with their oedipal implications)" (Kernberg 1993, 265). Such false bravado may be possible, but I think it is unusual, inasmuch as the propensity for shame can rarely be kept at bay for long. What *is* operant here is an extreme disavowal, which has a temporary cessation of empathic contact with the sexual object and leads to the dehumanizing experience: the "isolism" of the Marquis de Sade. Once again, then, we see how the split allows sexual conduct to overtake the personality temporarily. When the experience is transferred and reenacted in the transference, the analyst is able to participate in the patient's feelings of dehumanization and alienation, both as the patient himself has often felt them *and* as the patient assigns the role of being treated as a thing to the analyst. One must, I submit, recognize this not as a malicious or deliberate attempt to debase the analyst, but as a statement of an experience that lives on and is reenacted in analysis as a communication. The analyst often erroneously reacts to such a painful disregard of her humanity by interpreting the patient's hostility or by revealing its personal impact on her. Essentially, the latter reaction consists of an appeal to the patient's reality sector—a plea to be treated with respect. As I detail in chapter 9, this plea inevitably reenacts a trauma to the patient. It is the rare patient who is not aware of this clear mistreatment of his therapist and who does not therefore become angry at having his misdeed pointed out. The dehumanization of the analyst is seen as an effort to disavow the patient's positive feelings. Only the sexuality is allowed to be experienced in the struggle over the longed-for empathic connection to the other.

Here is another example: A patient arrived five minutes late for an appointment and said that he hoped the analyst would nevertheless allow the patient the full analytic session. When the analyst failed to do so, the patient left at the usual time. The next day, he reported having dreamed of hitting a golf ball onto the green but also of feeling disappointed that it "had no roll"— the hoped-for continued travel of the ball failed to materialize. The patient likened this to the previous session and to his disappointment that the analyst had chosen not to extend himself to accommodate him. He described the analyst as aloof, cold, and uncaring in this posture, much like his father, who also would not or could not extend himself for the patient. The next day the patient reported a dream in which he was fighting mad and swinging at someone; he was so enraged that it was almost unbearable. The dream reflected an instance of unfair treatment that he endured in his family when his younger brother sold family jewels that were common property and kept all the money for himself. When the patient complained to his sister and father, they dismissed him with a shrug. He grew angrier and angrier at this double insult of injustice and disregard of his righteous indignation and awoke in a rage.

The patient associated this dream to similar mistreatments that he had experienced during the day and to the five minutes of analysis that the analyst had not offered. In what was to him a clear disregard of the realities and niceties of analytic practice, the patient went on to say that only the analyst's personality, his neutral coolness, could explain his failure to compensate the patient for the lost time. Although the analyst felt called upon to explain to the patient again that the extra time was not owed and that one could not conduct a practice according to the arrival and departure of each patient, he did not voice this response. He also simultaneously wanted to assure the patient that he understood just how the patient felt, that he could certainly empathize with a wish to have more time, to have someone go that extra step and care more. Yet he did not offer this response either. It became clear that both responses were necessary because the patient was equally realistic in his expectations and was entitled to a response. The analyst's feelings of realism and aggrievedness paralleled the patient's own duality. Indeed, this coexistence of feeling is wholly distinct from a fantasy that emerges from repression and dominates the person by its presence. In that situation the interpretation of the fantasy, often against resistance, comes as a relief to the patient because his heretofore unacceptable wish can be revealed without guilt. One usually says what one feels with a knowledge of what it means. Yet this patient seemed to feel no guilt in the sector of entitlement at the time, and there seemed to be no expectation in the reality sector. To react with empathy to the patient's expectation of extra time or to grant his wish was seen by the analyst as a submission that could theoretically be transported to the realm of fecalization— if one were to follow a particular way of libidinizing of data—or to the realm of personal debasement if one were to employ an adversarial perspective. To remain with the patient's supposed subjective experience might be considered therapeutic, but it could likewise be read as a disregard of one's rights, privileges, and needs. If, on the other hand, one were to speak to the reality sector of the patient's psyche, there would be, not surprisingly, a reaction of resentment at the assumption that the patient is not perfectly aware of the unreasonableness of the wish. In a way, the analyst cannot win. Either he is the debased, humiliated, and possibly enraged person, or the patient is. Later I propose the proper or most desirable therapeutic stance in this sort of dilemma. Now, however, I focus on the hostility and assumed dehumanization that confronts the analyst here, which is inevitable and always shared.

It is of interest that the vignette I reported above occurred with a patient for whom sexualization was a common mode of reaction, especially in situations evoking painful affective responses. He rarely if ever felt, much less expressed, anger. The incident of righteous rage occurred after much analytic work. The angry reaction had a place and a justification both in and outside treatment. Transference reenactments that occur in the treatment of many cases of perverse behavior are distorted versions of parental mishandling or failures or are active traumas experienced vividly in the transference in this remarkable two-way manner, as both victim and victimizer. No matter how we may correctly and justifiably proclaim the analyst's innocence and noninvolvement, the inevitable and crucial revisiting of the patient's childhood involves a reciprocal experience for both partners in the dialogue. Especially in cases where sexualization has dominated one's affective life to the point of a near obliteration of shades of emotionality, we see upsurges of aggression and hostility as the sexualizing activity fades and recedes and as other emotions arise that are more appropriate to the circumstances. There are other cases in which the predominant mode of handling affective situations is one of chronic rage and the angry responses serve as a cohesive support to the self. These are different and do not represent cases of a newfound emotionality of anger.

Rather than equate perverse behavior with anger or insist that such behavior is always a dehumanizing process or that all sexual activity is designed to subjugate the partner and thus to express sadism, a better classification may be possible by unpacking the problem.

1. Normal Sexuality

The claim that polymorphous perverse infantile sexuality serves to recruit aggression in the service of love that characterizes human sexuality (Kernberg 1993, 253) can lead to the erroneous claim that there is a similarity between aggression in perversion and aggression in normal love relations (p. 252). I suggest that the aggression of perversion is more characteristically a rageful reaction to narcissistic injury or loss of control and is therefore an effort to redress grievances, which is more properly reactive. The wish to hurt, although present in some sexual conduct, is not part of normal aggression. Normal aggression is a joyful pursuit of a goal, an action at the behest of a cohesive self with an aim of success. It is not meant to inflict pain.

2. Two Forms of Narcissistic Rage

Here we follow Stoller and Kohut in distinguishing those reactions to trauma to the grandiose self and to a failure of the idealized selfobject. The yawning therapist illustrates the first reaction, and the analyst who held fast to the allotted time demonstrates the second. That these reactions may occur in sexual relations merely underscores the point made earlier about sexualization; that is, it reflects a vulnerable structure.

These forms of narcissistic rage are not specific to perversions, but the following category does seem to be more specific to these disorders.

3. Dehumanization

The dehumanization frequently said to characterize perversion must be differentiated as primarily a wish to eradicate emotionality (as in the patient who attempted to practice anonymous sex), from the approach that has a clear communicative intent. In well-conducted treatment the first state moves from initial noninvolvement to a display of victimization based on the two forms of rage discussed earlier. These forms are likewise the essence of the second state—that is, a communication of revenge for the traumas experienced as victimization during development. Treating someone like an insect may represent a feeling in one's self that was once induced by someone else. The range of reaction in the patient from a nonfeeling state to intense hostility may be a clue to an initial emergence of feeling rather than a guide to the severity of the supposed traumas of childhood. Therefore, the emergence of anger is not to be judged as a basic or fundamental hostility inherent in perversion that must either be discharged, tamed, or interpreted away, nor as an empathic failure of the therapist to remain a sustaining selfobject for the patient. Since the appearance of this form of anger is both necessary and inevitable, it is best not to regard it as anything other than welcome in treatment. That it often takes the form of a direct attack on the therapist allows one to pinpoint the initiation of the rage reaction better. With rageful responses of the patient comes an entry for both patient and analyst into the nature of the connective links that were once a part of the patient's repertoire and were subsequently replaced by sexualizations.

These entry points are also the foci for the effective treatment of the split self, which remains a characteristic of the patient and is especially dominant in the initial affective responses. This was noted in the patient whose rage reaction seemed isolated from his parallel feeling that his demand was totally unrealistic. What I am suggesting is that the sexualizations that seem to dominate the perversion and to exist in some form in all sexual activity give way to angry and rageful reactions after effective analytic or therapeutic interventions. The reactions of anger are seen in patients who have managed to obliterate their feelings through sexualizations until the problem is dealt with in treatment.

As an illustration of the beginning modification of both the anger and the split, I offer a dream of a patient who called and left a message asking to change an appointment a few days later. When he came for his regular appointment—after the call and before the hoped-for changed appointment—he reported a dream of discovering that a friend of his had come to town and had failed to call him. He was at first angry at this news but then told himself that he had been guilty of similar neglect of this friend on another occasion, so surely he could not reasonably be angry for long over this incident. The patient had many associations to the dream in terms of his anger with his father for failing to be a proper parent for him. He wanted to tell his father again and again that he held him responsible for his sad state of mental health. In a conversation with his brother, it had been suggested to him that this was all to no avail. When the patient also connected the dream to the analyst and the appointment request, he said he understood that he had been prepared to be angry, because he knew it was unlikely that another appointment time could be arranged and yet realized that his was an unreasonable request. He then puzzled over the fact that he could easily see himself in one or another of these mental states: of anger and of reasonableness and, indeed, he seemed able to go back and forth between them. Perhaps he was capable of being less angry because of the coexistence of the other state, just as there seemed to be an abatement of the rage toward his father alongside his brother's suggestion. He then announced that generally he felt he was getting more from the analyst these days than earlier in the analysis: more responsiveness, more answers, and more insight. He may also have been feeling less cut off from his father.

That such rageful reactions may also be part of so-called normal sexuality is probably explained in the same manner as all rage anywhere and everywhere—that is, as reactions of narcissistic injury to one or another of the poles of narcissism, which, of course, are exquisitely vulnerable during normal intercourse. One's grandiosity and need for a merger with an idealized object are essentially vulnerable during a sexual encounter and, not surprisingly, are prone to injury and reactive rage. Normal sexuality, in a sense, always has a component of aggression and may sometimes show evidence of sexualization and rageful reactions, but sexualization and rageful reactions cannot be considered normal unless we choose to equate common occurrence with normality. They are best thought of as pathological phenomena when they are part of perverse behavior and thus as representative of psychic disorder, although they are within the range of everyday living. To collapse all aggression into one concept is an error, just as to assign one meaning to all sexual behavior is a mistake.

A tested method of determining the true nature of aggression, rage, and dehumanization is, of course, to ascertain the nature of the unconscious fantasies that accompany the behavior. Just as an oedipal fantasy is to be expected in the aggression seen in normal sexual behavior, so one should expect rage reactions to reflect images of self-injury (as in the unfair treatment dream), failed ideals (as in the satellite dream), and vengeance. Still, the use of the hostile experience has a peculiar psychoeconomic effect of its own.

The Interplay of Sexualization and Rage

The patient who experiences intense hostility that was previously relieved or obliterated by a sexualization substantiates the interpretation of Stoller and others that perversion is an expression of hostility. These rageful reactions are connected to memories of selfobject failures in childhood relived in the transference and so may be judged to be the more genuine and the basic issue behind the perverse activity. Indeed, the patient may say that he now understands he has been angry all his life without really knowing it. Often the rageful feelings are short-lived, and we see once again the appearance and domination of a sexualization. A dream of hiding or walking away from the anger may appear. The position of sexualization as a defense is clear until the anger returns to claim center stage once again. It is peculiar that the anger has achieved the quality of firming and strengthening the self. On occasion, there are patients with chronic narcissistic rage (Kohut 1973), for whom anger does what sexualization does in perversion; that is, it substitutes for and defends against the experience of almost every other affect. Although one could say that the rage threatened a tenuous relation with the selfobject and necessitated a sexualization to retain a tie and forestall further regression and possible fragmentation, one could also say that the sexualization became so shameful and frightening that an angry reaction was needed to right the self and to correct the humiliation suffered by the unresponsive selfobject. What happens over time is an alternating between these states, with an effort to attain a reasonable condition of equilibrium. It becomes difficult to say what is primary, what is real, and what is defensive, what to interpret, and where to stop. Of course, such a quandary presents itself in much of analytic therapy, and the neatness we hope for is rarely evident. This does, however, reinforce the impression that a mixture or alternation of sexualization and rage is more the rule than is a clear demarcation between them.

What occurs after the appearance of these alternating moments of sexualization and rage is a gradual lessening of each along with a growing tolerance for both and the appearance of new forms and varieties of emotionality. It is not the case that one discharges and is relieved of the rage or the sexualization. Rather, each display or experience of these intense states represents a fragile self in need of further structuralization. The interpretation of one or another stormy emotional moment is never enough, because the need is more structural than cognitive; that is, the need is for a connecting and sustaining selfobject. The dehumanization must therefore be read as an attempt to make such contact, though in a form that is regressive, archaic, and reflective of earlier failed or thwarted efforts. The motive is not to devalue or to spoil. The rage is to be seen as reactive but also as temporarily shoring up of the self. Finally, the better integrated self becomes capable of acting in a more forthright and aggressive way. The aggression, differentiated from reactive rage, operates at the behest of a cohesive self. The structural filling in that is sought is difficult to attain. It is the matter to which I now turn.

9

An Overview of Treatment

Although the treatment of perversions by psychoanalysis or psychotherapy, individual or group, can be said to follow the ordinary rules and methods that apply to any form of such psychological interventions, there are special considerations that apply to these particular disorders. First, questions about perverse behavior are not usually part of a routine diagnostic interview. Patients with problems about sexual choice and behavior either present themselves with this initial complaint or reveal it, perhaps reluctantly, at some time during treatment. Determining the reason for the interviewer's hesitancy to bring up issues of deviant behavior is always interesting. It is not uncommon, and even therapists who obtain detailed sexual histories have difficulty in asking about sexual perversions. During treatment, a rather elaborate sexual scenario emerges for many patients, and, not surprisingly, pornographic material commonly accompanies such a revelation. The most unremarkable use of pornography is as a stimulus and accompaniment to masturbation as a nighttime sedative. Unusual and bizarre forms of perversions, on the other hand, are often brought to the therapist's attention at the start of the treatment, usually because of the patient's need to ascertain immediately the nature of the therapist's reaction to the disclosure. Whether the perversion is announced at the start of treatment or is revealed during treatment, every patient with perverse behavior wants to know what the therapist thinks about it. Whether the patient presents his action as desirable or despicable, it has a different standing for him than, say, depression or phobia, the symptoms of which are easily described as ego-dystonic or ego-alien and are often characterized as a foreign body or a mystery, something that has happened to the patient and that he or she would well be rid of. It is the rare patient who feels responsible for his or her neurotic symptom. In contrast, patients often feel culpable about their perversions. Even those who claim to be content with their perversions demand of the therapist an opinion and a stance.

Now, it is surely an easy solution for the therapist to claim neutrality with regard to such conditions as homosexuality, but that rapidly disappears with bestiality and pedophilia. The patient always makes an explicit or implicit plea to the therapist to position herself with regard to the behavior as acceptable or in need of eradication; the subtext of the patient's plea is that the therapist view the behavior as necessary versus (perhaps) dispensable. For no matter how much the patient may claim to wish to be rid of the problem, an equal case can be made for its continued existence. No matter how much the patient may claim to have made peace with the symptom and therefore to be able to live compatibly with it, there is somewhere a voice telling him to change or remove it. The shoe fetishist who presents his solitary ritual as an exercise in unalloyed pleasure begins treatment asking to be freed of his symptom but gives up treatment once he sees the efforts of the therapist directed to that goal. The cross-dresser who is told by a psychiatrist that his behavior is so rooted in his past and in his biology that he must learn to live with it insists that he is content with this conclusion but nevertheless decides to go into treatment just to see whether change is possible. Everyone, from the caricature of the happy heterosexual whose Don Juan life is the envy of his friends to the miserable abuser of animals, asks the therapist what he or she thinks of the behavior. They are *equally* pleased and mortified with the response because, unlike the neurotic patient who joins hands with the therapist to do battle with his depression, the patient with perversion knows that therapy will oblige him to confront the fact that the behavior cannot be removed or altered without unhappy consequences and that to remain locked in its persistent grip can be equally intolerable. Thus, treatment presents the patient with a dilemma not easily resolved.

Some perversions so dominate the personality that psychological intervention is not a likely tool for change. Those who do come for treatment, however, cannot help but ask about the stance of the therapist, and they need and want to know it; they are not interested in a neutral position whereby the therapist suspends judgment or avoids the point altogether. Although hedging is common among therapists and sometimes works, what is probably the best answer is to recognize both that the behavior is important and necessary and that this causes its own difficulty for the patient as well as others. The treatment must begin with the recognition of the split structure of the patient and so must not speak to only one or the other personality sector. If one empathizes with the subjectivity of the patient in and around the symptomatic behavior, one may lose sight of the reality factors involved. If one speaks only to the trials, problems, and negative effects of the behavior, one is allied with the sector of the psyche that always seeks to suppress the activity. The therapist who told a cross-dresser to call for an extra appointment when he had the urge to cross-dress unwittingly took the stand of opposing the symptom and was therefore, for a long time, barred from the forbidden actions of the patient, which had to be kept secret. But the therapist who asked to see the photos of his transvestite patient, as if in a position of acceptance, soon found himself embarked on a regressive trip that went beyond photos to videotapes, erotic letters, and so on to one as fraught with anxiety for the patient as it was with unrest and even disgust for the therapist. Neither silence nor siding with one or the other aspect of the split will work. Effective treatment must entail both aspects.

Kohut reports telling a patient who bragged of driving over the speed limit to reach his analytic appointment that he was about to hear the most important interpretation of his life. He then told the patient that he was a damn fool to speed and so risk his life. Therapists love that story, possibly because it reveals Kohut as being less the empathic listener of another's inner life and more the bearer of harsh reality. In fact, by coming down on the side of reality, Kohut did ignore that part of the patient that was demonstrating his eagerness, pleasure, and specialness as a patient. He made a choice to keep the patient alive, but it necessarily dampened or ignored the aspect that was equally in need of a response. At times the choice is easy, but at times we may choose too quickly or too decisively. In matters sexual, the choice may seem easier than it is. For example, Isay (1989) urges that homosexual patients be seen by therapists of similar sexual orientation. This becomes not merely a matter of the therapist's capacity to understand such a patient, but also of an agreed-upon and shared perception of the world. The gay therapist, one assumes, will no more seek to disabuse the patient of a homosexual choice than the honest and upright therapist would urge a patient to a life of crime. No competent therapist wants a patient to break the speed limit, because it is dangerous, wrong, and not in the patient's best interest to do so. Such a righteous stance is also attributed to the therapist who cautions a patient against a particular sexual behavior. The implicit message is that the therapist can somehow know beforehand what is in the best interest of the patient. Yet, it is more often than not the case that sexual behavior does not reveal its role in the psychological makeup of the person until some time into the treatment, so that the therapist simply does not know at the outset whether the patient's sexual behavior is good, bad, or irrelevant. In this she is on the same footing as the patient, who is equally ignorant of how his sexual behavior should be considered. This may also become confused with another issue, one involving rights and liberties. The initial decision in choosing a therapist becomes conflated in a debate about one's freedom to choose a form of behavior that is pleasurable and not injurious to others. This neatly and conveniently lifts the problem out of the area of deviance into the area of legality or morality. Such an exercise of depathologizing certain kinds of symptoms is not readily seen as the ruse it is, because by definition it is essentially an act of health. Yet if one suffers from sexual perversion, it can never be solely because of a code of morality. In chapter 1 I noted that society's view of deviation was at times important and at other times without relevance. So, too, our appraisal of any sexual behavior must be directed to its place in the psychology of the individual. A direction such as that of Isay, who advises the patient to seek a therapist who stands for a certain code of behavior, is often experienced as a foreclosure of options.

The condition of not knowing what is best for the patient is based on appreciating the duality of judgment that the patient lives with and experiences daily. Evelyne Schwaber (1992) makes an extended effort to understand the problem from the patient's point of view and to "relinquish the notion that ours is the more 'correct' truth when there is a difference between us and the patient about how we are perceived" (p. 1048). She urges a focus on the patient's psychic reality, how things are felt to be, and how they are perceived and experienced as true. She says, "Real is what each of us experiences as true, and the correctness of which no other one can be the arbiter" (p. 1042). This position essentially foregoes the claim of privileged access to reality. The existence of a patient's duality of judgment makes things more complicated since the patient does not enjoy a singular psychic reality on which to focus but rather lives with the same difference in perception that Schwaber uses to caution therapists not to impose their views upon the patient. Most of these patients are already doing that very thing to themselves. It is simplistic to think that a singular focus of the therapist is necessarily in the patient's best interest.

Perversion and the Technique of Neutrality

Lawrence Inderbitzen and Steven Levy (1993) present an excellent review of the analytic concept of neutrality in relation to interpretation and therapeutic intent. As salutary an effort as it is, it also speaks to the concept of the patient as a unitary subject. Whether one asks for a therapeutic stance equidistant from the ego, id, and superego or one closest to the ego (A. Freud 1965), the assumption for such neutrality is of a single psychic apparatus rather than the "side-by-side existence of cohesive personality attitudes with different goal structures, different pleasure aims, different moral and aesthetic values" (Kohut 1971, 183). To speak to one is possibly to injure the other. Indeed, this is why so many of the authors I have cited speak of creative solutions in perversions and of the need for a tolerance of the various paths potentially open to people (see chapter 1). One is readily moved to side with one or another aspect of the self, and one is regularly joined in agreement by that particular organized structure. As long as there is a connecting link to that particular side, the problem of equidistance and neutrality is easy, and the therapist can fairly readily achieve an empathic stance, a focus on the patient's psychic reality, and even recognition of his countertransference reactions. As we have already seen, in certain selected cases where a compensatory structure has formed therapists are able to ally themselves with that more stable organization and view the unstable and vulnerable other side as an interloper and troublesome. This view is also offered to us when the patient feels disgust or shame toward those disparate aspects of himself; this is often the moment when the therapist can speak to a reality sector as if it were a foreign and unwanted intruder. Still, even those cases betray the instability of the split inasmuch as there is often a lack of resolution and peace within the compensatory structure (as in the case of Michael), and what may compensate in terms of a defect can still lead to feelings of shame and guilt, as happens in many cases of homosexuality.

For the most part, however, the split ordinarily compels the therapist to side with rationality at times and to empathize with more infantile demands at other times. There is always an unpredictable quality to the shift from one side to the other, and it is usually impossible for the therapist to position himself properly for the optimal response to the needs of the split psyche. Commonly, perverse behavior is treated as something to be controlled or suppressed by methods varying from administering inhibiting biological substances to aversive therapy to efforts to place the behavior in a sequential line that can be understood causally—that is, you were depressed and therefore exhibited yourself. One therapist urged his patients to masturbate daily to diminish sexual pressure. Each of these stances is experienced as in opposition to the activity, and not surprisingly they often result in a diminution of the unwanted behavior. In a paradoxical way, however, a similar result may be seen when one refrains from any discussion of the perverse activity. This posture, which perhaps lays a better claim to neutrality, treats the symptom either as a necessary but unexplained bit of behavior that cannot be condemned or as something that is best ignored. At times this is as effective as efforts to control the behavior. Nevertheless, each needs to be explained since opposition and silence are of equal weight in suppressing the behavior.

The Sexualization Disappears

There is more than one reason for a relative decrease and ultimate disappearance of the sexualization; one (described in chapter 2) is structuralization and another is suppression. Depending on the nature of the connection to the therapist, either of these phenomena may temporarily dominate treatment. If the patient and therapist explicitly or implicitly take a stand against the appearance of an agreed-upon bit of perversity, a diminution or eradication of that symptom often results. The exhibitionist patient described in chapter 5 had had an analysis in which the symptom was seen alternately as due to a superego defect and to an inborn and therefore physiologically increased sexual tension. This was the patient who was a physician and was advised to masturbate before seeing his patients to alleviate the possibility of entering a situation with a patient that might prompt the symptom. This first analysis achieved some success in lessening the symptom, and, according to the patient, a concomitant generalized lessening of his anxiety allowed him to control the symptom more. This first episode of analytic treatment followed a legal action against the patient, and, in the second analysis, an arrangement was made to have another psychiatrist intercede with the legal authorities involved. This arrangement became an artificial device to relieve me, as the analyst, of responsibility or accountability for his behavior; therefore I had never felt that the patient had to control or suppress it. In cases where a silent agreement is reached that it is necessary to eliminate the symptom, it may well go underground for a while, but the message that usually emerges is the need for the patient to be allied with the therapist and for both to maintain constant surveillance.

For some patients the wish to please the therapist is a powerful incentive for compliance with a mutually agreed-upon manner of behavior, which one sees in a range of behavior from that of homosexuals who begin dating females to cross-dressers who burn all their female clothes and grow beards. Such compliant behavior, much like that involved in suppression, is realized in the sector of the self that is realistic and so aims to share the values and goals of the therapist. At this point in the treatment the goal of therapist and patient is to have reality dominate by strengthening the control of wayward impulses.

The relation of the therapist to the split-off and relatively unstructuralized sector of the personality fits the model proposed in my earlier statement on desexualization. The patient assigns a structural role to the therapist, who may, wittingly or unwittingly, accept that function. The vast majority of treatments, ranging from a twelve-step program to group therapy to aversion or behavior therapy to individual psychotherapy, all work to some extent for a period. They all fall within the diagnostic realm of narcissistic behavior disorders. If one is able to make and sustain such an assignment of structure filling (not building), it may well appear to be of lasting benefit as long as that person or persons—as therapist or group participants—remains in place. What occurs more often in psychotherapy is a modification in the status of the needed and available selfobject owing to regression and a transference issue that is not or cannot be responded to.

When the connection to a selfobject is made and there is a temporary filling in of the structural need, a relative state of stability is attained according to the position and level of the selfobject. Patients who sexualize need the unifying selfobject to aid in mastering excitement or overstimulation, as well as to "be something"—that is, to play the role in the dynamic equilibrium of the patient. Such a specificity of assignment (for example, to be a mother who mirrors the patient's accomplishments), starts one on a possibly regressive path: a path encouraged and made possible in analysis or one unattended to in other available treatments. Regression and the ensuing transference then become the arena for the necessary disruptions and reestablishments of empathy that make for the reappearance of the sexualizations. Thus, one must expect the waxing and waning of the perverse behavior, expressed as sexualization, during the course of treatment. This is the pivotal point of selfobject attainment, around which most forms of therapy are successful and then, after the inevitable selfobject failure, are doomed to falter. They fail because no structural change is accomplished. This is not to say that such inevitable failures are not equally expressed in a treatment that attends to these empathic connections, but such a treatment makes them the conditions for interpretations and so enables crucial points to become the essential base for the needed structure building. Unless this is the central issue of interpretation, the connections remain in the background. The feature of connecting is, for some patients with perverse behavior, a literal one. A patient dreamed of elaborate linkages, a "Rube Goldberg apparatus," or an elongated electric cord that could be plugged or become unplugged as an energizing and vitalizing connection from the analyst to the analysand was made and maintained or broken. The interpretations offered here are meant essentially to allow connections; they are not to be seen as unearthing hidden meaning.

There are treatments of sexual perversions that are nearly confined to the issue of the regulation and control of stimulation. It is this sort of case that I pointed to previously in discussing a rehabilitation of one pole that results in the formation of an effective compensatory structure. This emphasis may also be seen in a desexualization that once established can lead to an opportunity to modify a sexual orientation or to return to a previous state of adjustment. The content of these interpretations is initially centered on separations and absences and then on misunderstandings and empathic failures. Surprisingly, this is something that is ignored in many therapies, and, not infrequently, analysts and therapists join their patients in acting as though interruptions and holidays had little or no bearing on the conduct of treatment. Yet in almost all treatments of sexual perversions, the patient responds in anticipation of, during, and following all breaks in the continuity of the treatment, with an upsurge of sexual fantasies or activity. One should not, however, conclude that the interactions between patient and analyst are like a learning experience whose understanding will ultimately benefit the patient. Rather, they should be seen as a transference repetition that follows the patient's program in terms of the specificity and particulars of the reaction—that is, who leaves whom, who is in control, what is needed for reconstituting the relationship, and so forth. This is why and how disruptions are interpreted rather than mastered. Once again, I focus on the essence of cure as lying in interpretation. We can then move on to the particular qualities of the relationship.

Specific Issues beyond Tension Regulation

It is likely that acting out a sexual scenario and merely experiencing a fantasy without action can be differentiated on the basis of the form of the missing selfobject relationship. Kohut (1971, 47) distinguished three periods of disturbance in the relationship with the idealized object: (1) early ones that result in a general structural weakness and a diffuse narcissistic vulnerability (discussed in chapter 5); (2) later but still preoedipal periods that interfere with drive regulation; and (3) oedipal disappointments leading to incomplete idealization of the superego. The sexual perversions of action all have defects in the first and second periods of development. Those who are able to restrict their struggle to fantasied sexual behavior have achieved enough drive channeling and regulation to avoid handling the excitement and potential overstimulation by action. The earliest forms of disturbance, however, carry a clear message of sexualization as action, and much of the beginnings of treatment focus on the behavior's outbreak and recession. The split-off sector of the self operates in an impulsive and unregulated manner and is temporarily oblivious to ordinary superego demands. Those demands, however, may well exist in the parallel, realistic sector of the self. Thus, the acting-out pervert feels remorse or shame once that realistic sector is reengaged. So, too, a sexual fantasy often leads to shame or guilt after masturbation. Both the action and the fantasy represent defective idealizing selfobjects of different levels of maldevelopment; both are within the unneutralized sector of the self. Here, too, we see the defective grandiose self, and here is where an opportunity is available to differentiate one type of perversion from another on the basis of the particular form and developmental mishap of these two poles.

Before pursuing that goal, note that a sexual life previously confined to fantasy may, in theory, act out briefly under analytic regression. For the most part, however, this is not an issue, since the analytic selfobject relationship fits into or fills the structural defect, and the sexualization results from its ensuing failure or absence. Sexualization is brought to analysis as a device to forestall further regression, and the analysis should develop and concentrate around this feature. The question naturally arises whether interpretations are effective for disorders that have this early developmental origin and that might require a period of calm and regularity akin to a reparenting process. No doubt, conditions exist in which structurally vulnerable individuals find adequate and available selfobjects both in and outside treatment; they can then, therefore, pursue lives of relative stability. Once these selfobjects are lost, a structural vulnerability characterized by sexualization may then make its appearance. This period of stability with the selfobject presence of the therapist, however, is not to be taken as a goal in analysis or therapy, since it can be effective only as long as the fit of self and selfobject is maintained. Interpretations of and around the disruptions are necessary for any hoped-for improvement; to aim merely for a calming or settling effect is essentially only a start. Patients benefit from anticipating, knowing about, and thinking back on the sexualizations that result from and around empathic disruptions.

The Real Me

Fenichel (1945) tells us that the biological bisexuality of humans has three aspects: whether a person chooses an object of the same or the opposite sex, whether the sexual aim is to introduce a part of one's body into that of the object, and whether one has an active or passive attitude in life. He says that these aspects vary from one individual to another but that a certain amount of sexual feeling toward one's own sex remains in everyone (p. 329). Thus a man may behave in a manner that he feels to be feminine and may feel correspondingly good or bad or proud or ashamed of such behavior. Self-reflection is a continual monitor of how we think we appear to others and so feel about ourselves. At times we all feel that we embody one set of qualities or another, and although this may be as superficial as looking good or bad, beautiful or ugly, or fat or thin, it can be carried over to the image of a sexual configuration that is compelling and at times unnerving. The vertical split allows one to be of two sexual configurations, and so the two live in mutual relation with those in the environment who lend support to those explicit entities. A man who cooks dinner and cleans up afterward may feel like a woman but with no discontent. He may go on to a fantasy of being such a woman, and as the developmental course proceeds to actions of dressing and behavior, it demands of him a blindness or a reaction of embarrassment. This is not a case of a false self concealing a true one. In fact, the person is not only both man and woman but may be puzzled as to which self is the real one. But surely, each is real. The problem is solved not through domination but by integration. The problem comes about, as we have seen, by way of the disparity of visions that greet the child and does not allow integration. In treatment, the solution comes about only by recognizing the duality of the transference. Here there is another facet of interpretation, one directed to a disillusionment leading to a more realistic outlook and thus to a unification.

Healing the Split

The structural vulnerability I have noted, which is reflected in sexualization itself, is distinct from the vertical split, which is a different structural problem. Although the former condition allows for stability by offering a selfobject to help control, regulate, and forestall regression, the rift in the self demands a totally different psychological intervention. One can visualize the difference in the following adaptation of a diagram by Kohut (1971, 186) (figure 1).

A responsive selfobject that connects to the unmodified or unneutralized sector of the personality allows for a modulation of the fantasies and propensities to action in that area. If it is not available, a regressive move can result, allowing for sexualization. Such a selfobject is thus needed regularly and permanently because that sector is relatively unstructuralized and ever in search of sustaining selfobjects.

The split is different from structural vulnerability not only because it serves as an effective way to organize the psyche, but also because it is relatively stable and operant only as the need arises. As we have seen, the split ranges from the ordinary to the overtly psychotic. So, too, the phenomenon of sexualization is

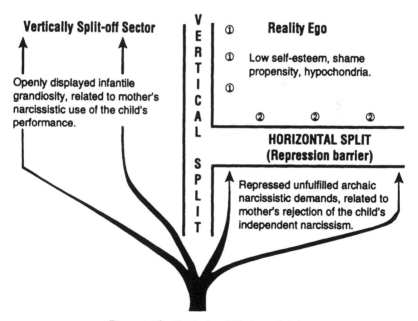

Figure 1 The Vertical and Horizontal Split

not and need not be tied to any of psychoanalytic particular diagnostic categories. Narcissistically vulnerable people may be realistic yet extremely hypersensitive and have difficulty in modulating affect. Their psychic structure bears no necessary correlation to the existence of a vertical split. The two are joined only in my characterization of perverse behavior, in which the split allows for the expression of sexualization in a manner seemingly unknown to the self.

Kohut (1971, 183) claimed that "the innumerable ways by which the increasing integration of the split-off sector is brought about defy description," noting only one: that of the patient describing his or her perverse activities. This example is a close cousin of the type of interpretations that are made about the occurrence of sexualization involving empathic disruptions; that is, they comment on behavior. One patient began analysis by insisting that he had no feeling whatsoever about his sexual performance but soon thereafter said that in talking of it he began to feel shame and remorse. Thus the gap begins to close. Though such patients start by seeing the world as black and white, they change and see the varied shades of affective experience. Yet the explanation lies not in the telling. That may confuse a result, which is the narrative, with a process, which is the structuralization. Figure 2 is a variation of figure 1.

In this illustration the available selfobject has a foot on both sides of the fence. I depart here from Kohut, who at one point felt that the side of openly displayed grandiosity was not to be considered as transference (1971, 226). Rather, the proper view of the transference is one of a shared but contradictory reality. I suggest that interpretations bridge the gap created by the split. They do so by reenacting the behavior in words, by commenting on the behavior with feeling. There are different explanations for this process such as moving from sensorimotor levels to higher cognitive ones, from phase-specific nontraumatic empathic breaks to transmuting internalization, from affect intolerance to affect tolerance without a holding environment, and so on. Ulti-

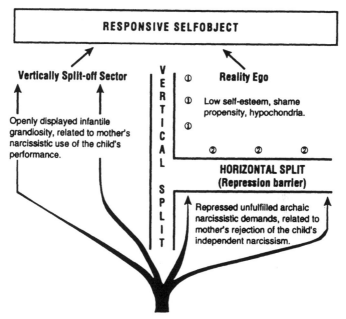

RESPONSIVE SELFOBJECT

Vertically Split-off Sector

Openly displayed infantile grandiosity, related to mother's narcissistic use of the child's performance.

VERTICAL SPLIT

① ① ① ② ② ②

Reality Ego

Low self-esteem, shame propensity, hypochondria.

HORIZONTAL SPLIT (Repression barrier)

Repressed unfulfilled archaic narcissistic demands, related to mother's rejection of the child's independent narcissism.

Figure 2 The Selfobject Bridges the Split

mately, it is the interpretation in the transference that allows for an in-depth integration of the crazy with the real; for example, the unconscious belief in the woman's penis (as a prototypical example) joins with a reality vision, and together they constitute the mixture of realistic attributes of a woman noted by Fenichel. The powerful mother is brought to a place on earth, not as a result of new learning, but as an effected integration of the two parts of what she was in real life.

The problem for the person with the vertical split lies in the unconscious fantasy of the phallic mother operating on both sides of the gap. The union, therefore, is not achieved by conscious realization and repudiation of that fantasy, as in one who has repressed it or split it off horizontally, but comes from allowing the untamed and unaltered vision to join with and so to modify the parallel but opposite counterpart. Undoing repression is said to relieve by way of insight and renunciation or judgmental condemnation (Gedo and Goldberg 1971, 145), while the disavowal is said to undergo "optimal disillusionment" (p. 169). This latter speaks too much of something the analyst is or does. The nature of interpretation here is one of integration of the two sides, which may, of course, be disillusioning to one side of the psyche but may also be enriching to the other. It is the mix that matters. For example, a patient told of having to switch from one fantasy to another for sexual stimulation as each became unusable as a result of his interpreting it. The end point of integration lies not in repudiating it, but in acknowledging and accepting what was once disavowed.

The Relation of the Split to the Structural Weakness

Since splitting is a common and prevalent phenomenon, it can be seen in otherwise well-structuralized individuals; that is, it lends a stability to the self even though one exists in a duality. Thus, when we are in a situation of anxiety, we may mobilize a more grandiose self to forge ahead into a potential danger situation (such as public speaking), or we may need a period of disavowal (as after the death of a loved one). These transient periods of disequilibrium are not situations of significant structural deficiency in one sector of the personality, although they do operate with relations of potential contradiction vis-à-vis the environment and selfobjects in the environment. One can, in theory, operate in such a duality for much of one's life. Only when there is also a significant structural weakness in one sector of the split do we see evidence of instability and, in particular, sexualization. The more adaptive sector of the personality reacts with a negative affect to much of the display of the structurally weak sector, but, again, this is not a necessary sequela of the combination of split and sexualization. It may be, therefore, that the treatment of the structural deficit will allow for the integration of the divided sectors at times while at other times a tolerance for that sector may follow. The tolerance or acceptance of an otherwise foreign aspect of the personality may lead to stability and may seem, for all intents, to be an integration. It often betrays itself, however, with an "It's not me" quality, one that coexists with anxiety but is still greeted with surprise. Yet another form of the stable coexistence of personalities of difference, such as in a sporadic perversion, is the ever-present tolerance with distaste: an acceptance of necessity. Therefore, when we consider the role of a compensatory structure, we should carefully weigh whether it has succeeded in integrating the personality or has merely mobilized sufficient satisfactory selfobjects to sustain the self while remaining at odds with the self as a whole. In other words, has it succeeded in rehabilitating a sector of the self without healing the split, which persists in an atmosphere of tolerance and compromise? True unification heals the split, and this is the particular role of interpretation in disorders that are not healed by compensation.

A Clinical Example

The technical management of these interpretations is often like a balancing act; the therapist is likely to come down too strongly on one side or the other. If she maintains a focus on the patient's perverse plight, she may err on the side of encouraging the action. An example is an incident from the analysis of a physician-patient who masturbated with or had fellatio performed on him by dogs, his children, or near-comatose patients. His initial shame subsided after the analysis began, as did much of his perverse behavior. The main content of the interpretations early in the analysis had to do with handling his excitement and over-stimulation. Early in the analysis it became clear that he was becoming excited by my interpretations. At first I took this to be a sign of his narcissistic vulnerability and the temporary over-loading of the system. I explained to him that the reason my statements frightened him was because they suggested that after an interpretation we could be more involved with one another and that this in turn overstimulated him. When I then missed a session because of a meeting, he acted out in his customary way with his dog. He realized that he enjoyed stimulating and exciting others and that trying to arouse someone otherwise unarousable was a feature of his perversion. Thus he felt that he was able to arouse or get a response from me. Stimulating others made him feel alive, and this activity was readily connected to the emotional absence of his father, a barbiturate addict. This connection was dramatically reenacted in one side of the transference; the interpretation was not integrative, however, since it addressed only the one side.

I cite this case as a possible example of a failure of mine as the analyst to empathize, of the outbreak of sexualization in the transference, and of how my own interpretive focus actually brought about the acting out. With the recognition that he was getting his excitement from me, the patient moved into a period of tiredness and depression. We then together went into an analysis of the father, who when on drugs was at times overexcited and at times lethargic. Both aspects participated in the analysis. The focus then shifted to the reality sector, which had been almost absent during the preceding episode. This commentary bridged the gap. The analysis could end successfully only in a unified self that integrated the two sides of the vertical split.

This vignette should demonstrate the need for interpretations to be carried over to the particular stories of our patients, that is, their mothers and fathers, and their individual meanings, the family dynamics. I point the reader toward this dimension, which is a crucial one, one that has so dominated the psychoanalytic study of perversions that now, perhaps, it can be safely deemphasized. I next illustrate the particulars of the individual narratives by unpacking what may seem to be a similar perversion. Once we consider the many other relevant factors involved, the great differences between these patients will be clear.

Two Forms of Fellatio and Their Interpretation

As an exercise in illustrating the forms of selfobject needs as well as the nature of the developmental defect, I describe two patients: one with an active perversion that involved inducing women patients to perform fellatio on him, and one with a fantasy of performing fellatio on a man with a distinct and particular physique, age, and demeanor.

The first patient, John (described in chapter 5), would exhibit himself to a woman; he revealed in his dreams and fantasies that either his penis was blistered or the woman suffered from a cleft palate. The sexual activity was designed to arouse the woman and ultimately to cure her, much as he had wished to arouse and bring joy to his depressed mother. Thus we postulate a defect in the mother's responsiveness to his exhibitionistic fantasies, experienced in the transference by a repeated need for recognition. Coupled with this defect was a flaw in his capacity to regulate, a preoedipal failure of the idealized selfobject, which allowed these impulses to be expressed in action. The two problems combined to produce uncontrolled excitement in exhibitionism. The second problem was recognized in the analysis by outbursts of sexualization during analytic absences paralleling his mother's depression and his father's hospitalization when the patient was seven years old.

The second patient had fellatio fantasies that took two forms: in the first, the patient was sucking the penis of a middle-aged man who was a "father figure" and from whom he wished to gain strength and knowledge. This fantasy followed analytic disruptions or failures that revealed the patient's wishes to get more information or guidance from the analyst. The patient would speak of wanting extra hours with the analyst after a weekend and being offered them by the analyst. That this remained in the domain of fantasy was an indication of a later, possibly oedipal failure of idealization and a lasting feeling of needing to be more

masculine. The second fantasy was of a woman performing fellatio on a man. The patient felt the woman was himself; in the
fantasy, he was interested in and concentrating on the pleasure
given to the man. This fantasy seemed to represent a need for
responsiveness, and in it the patient was a woman because his
mother and sister had been the family members who most demanded attention. He said that his father was like a clown in
front of others and that he himself worried about looking like a
woman when he had to speak to groups. In this regard, it is
interesting that the first patient had no doubt about his masculinity and never had a fantasy like this patient's second fantasy. Thus we see two defects that combine to give the second
patient a feeling of both homosexuality (his fellatio fantasies,
which connected him to a father who failed him) and unsatisfied
mirroring (the failure of the mother to mirror him, not from
depression—which was the case for the first patient—but rather
from the mother's own narcissistic needs).

At the risk of extreme oversimplification and possible distortion, I recast these behavioral episodes into psychoanalytic perspectives as follows:

1. The fellatio represents the connection to the other person,
   who, as a selfobject, achieves a sense of completion for the
   patient.
2. The *action* of the first patient versus the fantasy of the second
   enables us to pinpoint the source of the developmental problem in each man as a failure of the idealizing selfobject to
   control and regulate the excitement. The fantasy indicates a
   higher stage of development, allowing for control; the action
   indicates the need for control.
3. The masculine image of the first patient indicates that his
   gender was mirrored, but other forms of achievement failed to
   elicit the hoped-for joyous response from his mother and father. Coupled with the idealizing failure, he developed the
   perversion. The bisexual image of the second patient indi-

cates that his masculinity, as well as other bodily and psychic achievements, was not mirrored. He needed to arouse the man with himself as a woman and at the same time get something (strength and masculinity) from the man. His perversion remained at the level of masturbating while fantasizing.

4. Each patient had a split that allowed a freedom of behavior or fantasy with no evidence of repression and that allowed the emotional significance of the sexual scenario to be experienced only in retrospect.

In the sexual scenario of fellatio we see several things: what is needed to complete the self and make it whole, the fact that this is expressed in action or fantasy that cannot be controlled, and its capacity to coexist with the person who may abhor it. In treatment, therefore, we need to establish a selfobject relation that controls the sexualization, interpretations that heal the split, and reconstructions of the childhood origins of the sexual scenario. The relation, the regulation, and the healing, however, each require individualized interpretation in order for the structuralization to take place.

The goal of treatment is an integrated self, which calls into focus such words as *whole, functional,* and *continuous.* The problem of perversion is its undoing of these states, with the result that the self is torn apart, unable to reach its goals, and is equally out of touch with itself. Yet the perversion is also an effort to keep the self together. Such efforts, however, can never lead to integration, because—at least in those disorders that we can hope to help—the wayward self is always at odds with the rest of the personality. That internal dissent is necessary for effective therapeutic intervention; it would be folly not to search for it in all perverse behavior disorders, or alternatively, to assume that it is but another source of pleasure that some may find personally unwelcome. Initially, it may be denied, but the split-off part at some point in the treatment is felt to be alien and is later welcomed back to the integrated self in a different form.

Finally, I would like to clarify the position of perversion as a narcissistic behavior disorder that characterizes a vertical split from those other forms of pathology that involve either one or both of the phenomena of behavior and splitting. When Freud (1909) discussed the superstitions of the Rat Man, he gave us a description of a person who was consciously aware of doing something he felt was strange or unexplainable. This became the prototype for a person involved in a seemingly personal contradiction of peculiar or irrational behavior, that is, a compulsive behavior disorder that in the Rat Man was accompanied by obsessional thinking. The crucial differentiating point here is that such behavior was experienced in and with a unity, that is, by an integrated individual. The coexistence of feelings in one person, feelings that range from this type of compulsive behavior to that of the division between the experiencing ego and the observing ego are examples of such a unity. There is no vertical split. In the split posited by Kohut (1971) in narcissistic personality disorders we see a division of the self into two parts, each with different experiences, albeit in an effort to maintain a unification. A grandiose self, for example, lives apart from the self of reality. The essential unity is lost, although both experiences are part of a self and are conscious. The self is split but not shattered.

This vertical split needs to be differentiated from the horizontal split of repression, which separates unconscious or inaccessible material. The thoughts and fantasies of a narcissistic personality disorder are disavowed but accessible. Although the feeling of unreality that may accompany such fantasies is often a sequence of the denied experience, it is conscious. This becomes even more apparent in the narcissistic behavior disorders whereby the vertically split-off sector is a participant in behavior that may be maladaptive. Such behavior is clearly to be distinguished from the compulsive behavior that characterizes the neurotic, whose self is essentially unified, as well as from the self suffering from a personality disorder, whose symptom is not translated into action. The conscious availability of the split-off vertical sector of narcissistic behavior disorders in such a person may also be a differentiating feature from other disorders; as is said to be true of multiple-personality disorders, dissociated personality sectors remain unconscious except in special circumstances. The range is thus from compulsive, irrational *behavior* in a unified person to disavowed, conscious *fantasies* in a vertically split person to disavowed, conscious *behavior* with a vertical split. The feeling of unification achieved by the vertical split avoids self-fragmentation, but it is not the essential unity of the unsplit self of the compulsive person. Figure 3 illustrates the differences:

1. Compulsive behavior: unified person with mixed feelings

"I do these crazy things all the time and feel silly."

2. Narcissistic personality disorder: vertical split with fantasies

"I feel lethargic and/or overexcited by my disavowed grandiosity, but it is almost like another person."

3. Narcissistic behavior disorder: vertical split with action

"I act out my disavowed sector and feel guilty or ashamed at what I have done as if it were by another person."

4. Dissociated personality— "Another, hidden person takes over my body and then disappears."

10

Deconstructing Perversions and Reconstructing the Self

I would like to have entitled this book "The Cause and Cure of Perversion," but I have had to settle for a more modest goal. I have always felt that perversion holds a unique position in psychopathology: as a behavior disorder that is often accompanied by much shame and guilt, as a supposed psychological difficulty that shares an equally problematic moral position, and as a study in psychoanalysis that defies consensus as to its status. Yet it is hard to pinpoint perversion. It is not a coherent category. As we have seen, opinions about it range from its being a reverse image of neurosis to its being found in typical neurotic personality organizations; from being basically biological to wholly psychological; its derivation as totally in castration anxiety to just as wholly lying in hostility; from its position as a disease entity in its own right to its existence being determined only by its perception in a social setting, and on and on. The best way to get a handle on perversion is to circle it slowly to see its changing shapes and forms. Through the method of multiple perspectives, one can start to break down the problem into particular areas, slowly taking it apart without destroying it or eliminating it.

Explaining Perversion

The usual explanations in any discipline have to do with causes or sequences. Science aims to explain phenomena by demonstrating what the determinant of an event is. The steel in some tires makes them wear-resistant, and low temperatures cause water to freeze. Thus we connect cause and effect. To explain perversion in this way, we need to show what, if anything, went wrong in childhood and explain whatever biological factors are relevant (or one day may be relevant). The problem psychoanalysis has in framing explanations for perversions concerns laying out sequences that, though they may tell a coherent story, lack the conviction of certainty. The best we are able to do is to form an explanation by description. We are unable to forge the tight links enjoyed by much of science in terms of neat causal chains. Ideally we should, and perhaps one day we shall, be able to correlate a particular moment in development, a special area of the brain, or even a crucial form of environmental trauma that leads to the child's discovery of and use of sexualization to handle his or her anxiety.

Even though we may now be able to assume that several factors come together that allow perversion to emerge, its single necessary cause may still be lacking. Without that we can only fall back on such ideas as subtle or unconscious parental encouragement or a significant chronological age, along with biological givens and even happenstance. We put them all together to do the job of explanation, but it serves only as a holding action until the fateful discovery of the real cause. Perhaps we would be better served by improving our available skills to describe the state of affairs that exists in perversion formation and rest content with that compromise—if indeed it is a compromise. This may be all we will ever attain—the best description possible.

Thus far, my descriptive explanations have centered on the developmental problems in self-formation and particularly those of the two distinct forms: a vertical split of the self and a structural defect in both idealization and grandiosity. The split allows for the coexistence of the self of perversion and a reality self. The failure of the idealized selfobject probably leads to the propensity for the start of sexualization, and, along with the associated failure of the mirroring selfobject, gives the perversion its particular form and content. Both poles of the self are structurally defective, and this is likely added to an existing generalized narcissistic vulnerability. These, therefore, are the three basic ingredients of perversion: the sexualization of the self, a split in the self, and the oscillation of problems in idealization and grandiosity that make for the individual story in the development of the self.

This framework provides a template that enables us to explain the individual patient who manifests perverse behavior and to follow a treatment course that will help us to organize the clinical data that emerges. That we need such an orienting framework is confirmed by the way we conduct our treatment, the way we choose what needs to be attended to versus what can be put to the side. It is never a case of allowing clinical material to emerge and then following it. Presumably people listened before Freud came upon the scene, and those listeners had no idea where they were heading. We must know what to listen for.

Explaining perversion this way allows us to claim that a person manifests perverse behavior because of three conditions and that no one without these psychological factors will have the problem of perversion. It thereby takes us further toward understanding perverse behavior by recognizing what constitutes it exactly or allows for its existence. The explanation at this point serves only as a framework that requires filling in by interpretation. To be sure, one can claim that nothing, including our explanatory framework, is entirely free of interpretation; but for psychoanalysis this has a special meaning. Interpretation of the perversion adds the varied forms and configurations of perverse behavior to this explanatory grid.

The Interpretation of Perversions

Humans are interpreting animals; we do not all see things in the same way. From the fundamental notion of observing the simplest object to the complex consideration of a theoretical idea, there seems always to be a contribution from the observer. Apples do not appear the same to all of us, because each of us brings our experiences to our view of the apple, and certainly a concept such as democracy is inevitably laden with personal prejudices and convictions. The way we see things, the preconceptions we bring to each and every consideration, and the ongoing processing of vision and examination are the stuff of interpretation. Perversions look different to different people and may even change their status from normal to deviant according to the interpreter. Every perversion is a product of what it is and what it does to another.

Interpretation is in vogue these days, fashionably considered a hermeneutic activity that is studied both from a philosophical and a literary viewpoint. In the process of interpretation an observer or interpreter views an object, text, or another person and brings his or her prejudice to bear upon the studied phenomenon. A to-and-fro process then takes place as the interpreter aims to complete her expectations from the perception or study of the object, which subsequently demands feedback and a corrected interpretation. That is what we need to do in the study of perversion. Since the conclusion of correctness is so dependent on the initial bias of the observer, it is unlikely that a single, correct interpretation will be arrived at by several observers; thus hermeneutics must carry the criticism of being more often than not a matter of opinion rather than fact.

To answer this charge, some analysts invoke the ideas of literary critic E. D. Hirsch (1967), who claims that interpretations can be tested, confirmed, and agreed upon. This view lends itself to the claim that there are indeed correct interpretations and that we can somehow gain access to the proof of such correctness. Freud (1912) gave us a method for determining the validity of interpretations, but the problem has grown. We must distinguish the correct from the incorrect, as well as recognize that correctness is not singular; there are many correct versions.

In contrast to Hirsch's viewpoint, Hans-Georg Gadamer (1965) claims that a fusion of horizons between the interpreter and what is being interpreted, or between one person and the person one is trying to understand, necessarily and inevitably changes both parties. Thus interpretation is not the study of a static or fixed object, but a process of the creation of shared meaning. For perversion, it is a question of the slipperiness of certainty about its status and existence as it shifts from one theoretical perspective to another and from one interpreter to another. Now, however, we are constrained by the explanatory framework we have fashioned.

Interpretation in psychoanalysis aims to add a dimension of observation that is unavailable to the untrained person. Here is where one explanation gains precedence over another. Interpretations are always of multiple and varied perspectives, since in pursuing the visual model the trained eye knows what to look for, and the ignorant eye is blind. Psychoanalytic interpretations, however, carry an added layer of impenetrability to the casual observer, since they are said to be actively hidden from normal view. When we subscribe to a particular way of ordering data, seeing sequences, and noting phenomena, we interpret according to these preexisting beliefs. These prescriptions then become guides to proscriptions: they tell us where to stop. As Ludwig Wittgenstein said, "What happens is not that this symbol cannot be further interpreted, but: I do no interpreting. I do not interpret, because I feel at home in the present picture." Feeling at home makes it right, and we stop.

There has been no such comfortable resting place for perversion. The interpretation of perversion has become a playground of psychoanalytic guesswork. At times it reads so harshly that the problem seems less one of pathology than of evil. Perverse behavior is never what it seems to be; it always stands for something else, and that something often appears to be outside the realm of humanness. As we have seen, there is a strong tendency to stress the hostile and cruel intent of the perverse person, to characterize the pervert as one who dehumanizes, and also to insist on the elimination of the symptom.

No perversion occurs in a vacuum, and our interpretations of perverse behavior aim to reveal it to be a form of communication of something to someone. When we ourselves use interpretation it takes on a new and special meaning. There is, of course, a twofold sense here to interpretation: the first has to do with the way we perceive and decode an act of perversion to determine what the behavior is trying to say—to communicate outside language; the second is the use we make of interpretation when we deliver our comprehension of something to a patient. The first is framed by our ways of explanation; the second is motivated by our therapeutic intent. The first is the message we feel the perverse behavior delivers to the world, one that lives outside language, while the second is our effort to use language so that it may transform the action of the patient into a new capacity: ideally, a capacity to self-reflect.

Therefore, we insist upon interpretation not only because it helps us to close the circle on perversion, but because it is our primary tool. No matter what may happen in therapy or analysis that seems helpful to the patient, we should be wary of efforts to dismiss interpretation. We must attend to what we know happens in the analytic encounter, whether it be a smile, an instruction, or a lapse. The nature of treatment and analysis is not to rely solely on the noninterpretable interaction, because that will happen anywhere and everywhere, and in that sense, we are no different from friends, teachers, or anyone else. We are distinguished only because we can interpret, and that is what gives us the meaning of what we do and what our patients are. Interpretations not only expose what has been hidden but create new configurations of meanings. They affect all three levels of the self, and they therefore deal with all three problematic areas in perversions: the split, the structuralization, and the story.

Until now, the interpretations available for decoding perverse behavior have been restricted to psychoanalytic ideas about the Oedipus complex, castration anxiety, and the element of hostility. One therefore built up a story about a single individual with the constraints of that set of expectations or preformed ideas. We stopped interpreting when we, as Wittgenstein said, felt at home with our conclusions. By insisting on the many ways that the oedipal conflict can be played out, we have been able—since Freud and Fenichel—to allow for many individual scenarios, but it soon became clear that such interpretations were not wholly effective in the treatments of these or other behavior disorders. The answer to this limitation has at least two possibilities. The first says that you have got the story wrong; you need another story. Here is where preoedipal factors come into play, and that is where the new story of self psychology can make a claim. The second answer asks that we change our ideas about interpretation in order to move away from the idea of exposure (the archaeological model) and move closer to Gadamer to see how interpretation changes the participants and to explicate the nature of sharing a meaning. Now we move to the meaning of perversion.

The Meaning of Perversion

Meanings connect us to the world. When we speak of what something means or means to us we are making a reference, essentially pointing to that thing, person, or situation. The words we use direct attention to these things, which are, in turn, the composition of the world we inhabit. The crucial point of meaning resides in the impact of the inhabitants of a person's world upon that person. It is what a thing does to you and how it moves you and touches you that determines what it does or does not mean to you. When someone speaks to you, she talks about her world in the broadest sense about the constraints of her personal universe. As you interpret the meaning of these utterances, you learn about that person's world, and you then know her better.

Meanings in psychoanalysis are, however, different in other fields. To attribute the meaning of a perverse action to a person is to say that he is living out a connection to someone else, a connection she is not aware of. She lives it out without clarity. It is the opaqueness of meanings that interests psychoanalysis, and unmasking them according to established principles is the basis of its activity. Many meanings are hidden and need uncovering; clearly part of the action of interpretation is to expose a meaning that is not readily apparent or available to perception. Foreign language interpreters, art historians, and car mechanics can tell us what particular verbal sounds or noises mean, but psychoanalysts must combine their interpretive and explanatory abilities to deliver hidden meanings according to their models and theories. Such models explain the unavailability of clear meanings as due, for example, to hidden oedipal wishes. The manner in which meanings are hidden and then exposed is the special province of psychoanalytic theory. Shaping and forming meaning for others by putting experiences into words is a common activity in many disciplines. Language is not the singular bearer of meaning; explanations in music and art often connect to the world by wordless means.

Perversion operates outside language yet is said to communicate. That is why the interpretations of psychoanalysis carry meaning that goes beyond the representative words to other issues, such as tension regulation, reality testing, and the experience of unification that furthers the work of interpretation in the formation of meaning. To discover what it means to participate in perverse behavior we must share a life that might offend us. We may feel strongly about the action of a pedophile on an innocent child, but we must also see what that action means to the offender; that is, we need to make an effort to connect to a selfobject. The meanings of perverse behavior make better sense when, by using our template of explanation, we see how we may fit into another person's self structure—that is, as a selfobject. These person-to-person connections, of self to selfobject, are strikingly unavailable to the sexualizing person, who is continually unable to complete a stable self vis-à-vis the world. The connections are unavailable, they are faulty, they lack the necessary qualities of humanity, and so they are ever reflective of the pathological meanings of the perversion. As I have noted, if we succeed in finding our place in the psyche of the other, then we have moved to the level of understanding. The meanings that are formed create new connections to others and so lead to another psychological state.

Understanding Perversion

Understanding connects us to one another. Its subcategory, self-understanding, connects us to ourselves. It is this that underscores all the understanding of meanings, interpretations, and explanations that we achieve. Self-understanding is a form of separating off a part of us, contemplating it, and integrating it into the whole. To understand someone else is an aspect and a result of communication; to understand oneself comes from self-reflection.

We understand someone by reading that person, usually by way of empathy. This much abused word is carefully described by Basch (1983) as the final stage in a line of affective development, a form of communication in a hermeneutic circle. He says that "an affective experience of one's own is first identified as a response to or resonance with another; this leads to a reasonably though not necessarily conscious interpretation of what this means or says about the other; this postulated conclusion about the other's mental state is then subjected to validation or disconfirmation by testing it against reality through further reflection, observation, or experiment" (p. 111). Kohut described empathy as "vicarious introspection," a phrase that locates the field of study within the observer, who somehow lifts the state of the other into herself.

Psychoanalytic understanding involves the method of achieving it, the reason to aim for understanding someone else, and the explanation of what the understanding does to us. If raising unconscious material to consciousness leading to insight serves as a model of self-understanding, then an analytic model of the psyche will give us a picture of the process. If, as self psychology posits, the nontraumatic empathic breaks followed by interpretations that lead to structure formation are subsequently regarded as responsible for self-understanding, then another type of model may serve us. Each model has a picture of a psychic alteration and thereby allows for the understanding of psychoanalysis to stand apart from, for example, that of a mathematical equation or of the rules of a game. For many people the task of empathizing with a pedophile or a fetishist is so uncomfortable that they choose a position of scientific detachment. Such a stance excludes treatment, which demands a connection.

Sequencing

The beginning encounter with a patient is devoted to gathering data by observing and listening. This is the start of the hermeneutic circle and the effort to understand, which, as I have said, is a stage of empathy and includes all the affective components, preconceptions, and prejudices the observer brings to the study. Of course there is no such thing as "pure" listening, listening without the baggage of theories and prejudices that any reader brings to a text or any therapist to a patient. One looks for and listens for hidden meanings. The understanding of the patient that is achieved by way of empathy is directed toward those meanings. It is true that an area of understanding occurs for any two people in conversation, but understanding becomes analytic only when the hidden meanings belong to one's model of analysis. Understanding and empathy, whether brief or sustained, do not constitute an analytic stance without a psychoanalytic perspective—for example, a belief in the unconscious. Only within this understanding can we see and interpret the world of the patient and significant connections according to our psychoanalytic models. Those meanings that emerge from hiding and that are constructed, if communicated, are meliorative because they lend themselves to increased self-understanding or increased psychic structure, or both. Hidden meanings, once exposed, and new meanings, once composed, allow for new connections to the world of the patient. Although this is the result of the interpretations offered to the patient, everything that is observed is initially subjected to our own interpretation, and only a small amount of what is interpreted is delivered to the patient. Thus we have the first qualification: we understand the patient according to our theories. We approach every study of perversion with many such preconceptions.

Though we understand by way of interpreting the behavior and associations of the patient, the practice of psychoanalysis merely begins there. The technique of analysis goes into communicating to the patient that he or she is understood, that we know what is meant, and that we can interpret new and hidden meanings. Being understood is a state akin to the ownership or appropriation that takes place when one understands anything at all; that is, it is a connection or expansion of the self or another person, a sharing of meaning. Thus, one's world changes when one understands or is understood; the set of connections or relations is altered, and one has a different sense about such relations. In the vocabulary of logic, the sense and the reference of things have changed. Thus the sequence goes from data gathering, to the interpretation of meaning, to the understanding and communication of understanding.

Sequencing Illustrated

At one point during his treatment, a man with perverse behavior noticed that he felt different about a time and occasion in which he had previously acted out. That this changed feeling was gradual was apparent to him, but in that particular session he contemplated it in an almost philosophic mood. His excitement and interest in the sexual activity seemed to be lessened, and he had mixed feelings of regret and triumph about this. He no longer felt a separation in his life between the self of perversion and the one he felt to be more appropriate. He had had a dream of picking up what he thought was his raincoat, only to find it much too small and tight for him. He then tried on a less attractive coat that was a bit large but certainly would do. He saw this dream as his passage from one form of life, one adaptation and persona, to another. The session occurred after he had also achieved a kind of reconciliation with his aging father and, in so doing, had also gained a sense of decisiveness about his sexuality. We could explain this change in him as a healing of his split and an increased structuralization, which diminished his sexualization. The dynamics of his relation to his faulty idealization of the father gave this man's story its individuality. Our shared interpretation of the dream enabled us to see him and to appreciate his new self-configuration together. As his life changed, the world became a different place for him, and the meaning of the things of the world were changed.

There are those who belong to the school that discounts or even deplores theory and insists on the magical ability of clinical material to deliver meaning. Many nonanalysts might find the jargon and theory of psychoanalysts jarring and would prefer to hear the patient's words and the therapist's responses, but our theoretical terms not only guide us and constrain us, they open our eyes. The concepts of sexualization and vertical splitting are convenient handles for organizing data, and with them an analyst will never see patients in the same way again.

The Reconstruction of the Self

Kohut's first book, *The Analysis of the Self* (1971), is a detailed inquiry into the forms of transference that developed in certain narcissistic personality disorders. It deals with analysis in the true sense of the word inasmuch as it focuses on transference (although of a new type) and its subsequent working through and resolution. His next book, *The Restoration of the Self* (1977), highlights the ways in which an undeveloped or a shattered self

can be restored. Kohut chose his words and especially his titles
with great care to avoid misunderstanding and to familiarize the
reader with these special words and definitive meanings. So, for
example, he did not choose to *repair, reorganize,* or *treat* the self,
but rather to *restore* it. The title of his last book, *How Does Analysis Cure?* (1988), was designed to emphasize his continuing
concern with the puzzle of how interpretation could allow the
undeveloped to develop, restore a shattered self, and add whatever the structure required, together with the insight gained.

Narcissistic behavior disorders, of which perversion is an outstanding example, supply the impetus to use reconstruction to
change a self that is both undeveloped and damaged. A person
who has developed a stable compensatory structure is one for
whom a new construction is not feasible; that is, there is no need
for a reconstruction, because a stable structure is in place. For
those whose self is poorly or irregularly constructed, who show
the split and sexualization of perversion, and for whom treatment is advisable, a new construction is called for. The process
is not a return to a previous state of stability or an allowing of a
freedom of development that was unavailable before. In fixing
things that are broken we must often go beyond restoration. The
structure I have examined in this book is a deficient one and
therefore requires a reconfiguration that allows for the regulation of excitement, the modulation of affect, and the achievement of functional harmony. The self is split, and the experience
and stability of unification require selfobject availability. We
must therefore move on from the deconstruction of perversion in
order to understand the phenomena of the reconstruction of the
self better and so treat it.

The concept of reconstruction is radical because it implies
dismantling something and erecting a new structure. It flirts
with the idea of an end point of design, an aim of achieving what
the therapist thinks is best for the patient. It brings to bear a range
of considerations about normalcy and morality, issues that we

try to put aside in discussions about perversion, but these issues can never be wholly ignored. We become the architects of personality as well as the healers of disease. For Kohut, analysis was constrained to undo damage, to restore what was broken; the analyst was then to step aside to allow the program of development to proceed according to inner or innate schedule. He certainly was to stop short of any effort to undo a compensatory structure. Not only was the task impossible, but the structure was inviolate. The next move in analysis seemed to require going beyond analysis, and here Kohut demurred.

Yet the next step can remain faithful to the analytic tool of interpretation while still enabling a newly constructed or restructured self to be possible. We can add the structuralizing role of interpretation to the old archaeological one since we can now see that the selfobject connection is the new locus of growth. The growth, however, is neither in a direction determined by the analyst nor is it that of a development not given a proper chance to resume its course. Perhaps if we see the multipotential of the self, we can allow for the middle ground: a growth responsive more to one selfobject or to one form of selfobject than to another, and particularly to a self of unification. I offer that as the next frontier for self psychology and the reconstruction needed for the proper treatment of perverse behavior disorders.

My effort in this book has been to explain and interpret perversion. Many interpretations have been offered for it, including everything from a moral failure to a statement of political freedom. The hardest job of all is to understand it—not as an entity apart from us, but as a part of someone's life that is inescapably a part of us all.

There is no simple or single cause of this class of disorder, but it is not so complex or chaotic that it cannot be encompassed. The process involved in doing so is that of the hermeneutic circle, or what Paul Ricouer called *appropriation*, by which one is broadened by a new self-understanding. No better result or greater benefit of this sequence of approaching the problem of perversion could occur than that of appropriation. The task of understanding perverse behavior is to make the necessary connection, to become part of the person's life, and so, inevitably, to become different ourselves.

References

Adair, M. J. 1993. A speculation on perversion and hallucination. *International Journal of Psychoanalysis* 74(1): 81–92.

Alexander, F., and Ross, H. 1952. *Dynamic Psychiatry.* Chicago: University of Chicago Press.

Alpert, A. 1949. Sublimation and sexualization: A case report. *Psychoanalytic Study of the Child* 3/4:271–78.

American Psychoanalytic Association. 1986. Panel report, Toward a further understanding of homosexual men, by Richard S. Friedman. *Journal of the American Psychoanalytic Association* 34(1): 193–206.

Bak, R. C. 1973. Being in love and object loss. *International Journal of Psycho-analysis* 54:1–8.

Basch, M. F. 1983. The perception of reality and the disavowal of meaning. In *Annual of Psychoanalysis* 11:125–54. New York: International Universities Press.

———. 1988. *Understanding Psychotherapy.* New York: Basic Books.

Bergman, M. S. 1971. Psychoanalytic observations on the capacity to love. In *Separation-Individuation,* ed. J. B. Mc Devitt and C. F. Settlage, 15–40. New York: International Universities Press.

Blos, P. 1991. Sadomasochism and the defense against recall of painful affect. *Journal of the American Psychoanalytic Association* 39(2): 417–30.

Blum, H. 1973. The concept of erotized transference. *Journal of the American Psychoanalytic Association* 21:61–76.

Boesky, D. 1988. Comments on the structural theory of technique. *International Journal of Psycho-analysis* 69:303–16.

Brandchaft, B. 1993. To free the spirit from its cell. In *Progress in Self Psychology* 9:209–29. Hillsdale, N.J.: Analytic Press.

Chasseguet-Smirgel, J. 1984. *Creativity and Perversion.* New York: W. W. Norton.

———. 1986. *Sexuality and Mind: The Role of the Father and the Mother in the Psyche*. New York: New York University Press.

———. 1991. Sadomasochism in the perversions: Some thoughts on the destruction of reality. *Journal of the American Psychoanalytic Association*, 39(3): 399–415.

Coen, S. J. 1981. Sexualization as a predominant mode of defense. *Journal of the American Psychoanalytic Association* 29(4): 893–920.

Edelson, M. 1986. The hermeneutic turn and the single case study in psychoanalysis. *Psychoanalysis and Contemporary Thought* 8(4): 567–614.

Fenichel, O. 1945. *The Psychoanalytic Theory of Neurosis*. New York: W. W. Norton.

Freud, A. 1965. *Normality and Pathology in Childhood*. New York: International Universities Press.

Freud, S. [1905] 1957. Three essays on the theory of sexuality. *Standard Edition* 7:125–245. London: Hogarth Press.

———. 1909. Notes upon a case of obsessional neurosis. *Standard Edition*, vol. 23. London: Hogarth Press.

———. 1911. Psychoanalytic notes on an autobiographical account of a case of paranoia (dementia paranoia). *Standard Edition*, vol. 12. London: Hogarth Press.

———. 1927. Fetishism. *Standard Edition*, vol. 2. London: Hogarth Press.

———. 1940. An outline of psychoanalysis. *Standard Edition*, vol. 23. London: Hogarth Press.

Friedman, R. C. 1986. Toward a further understanding of homosexual men. *Journal of the American Psychoanalytic Association* 34(1): 193–206.

———. 1988. *Male Homosexuality*. New Haven: Yale University Press.

Gedo, J., and Goldberg, A. 1971. *Models of the Mind*. Chicago: University of Chicago Press.

Glover, E. 1932. The relation of perversion-formation to the development of reality sense. In *On the Early Development of Mind*. New York: International Universities Press.

Goldberg, A. 1975. A fresh look at perverse behavior. *International Journal of Psycho-analysis* 56:335–42.

———. 1981. Self psychology and the distinctiveness of psychotherapy. *International Journal of Psychoanalytic Psychotherapy* 8:57–70.

———. 1988. *A Fresh Look at Psychoanalysis: The View from Self Psychology*. Hillsdale, N.J.: Analytic Press.

———. 1990. *The Prisonhouse of Psychoanalysis.* Hillsdale, N.J.: Analytic Press.

Hartmann, H. 1964. *Essays on Ego Psychology: Comments on the Psychoanalytic Theory of the Ego.* New York: International Universities Press.

Inderbitzen, L., and Levy, S. 1993. Neutrality, interpretation, and therapeutic intent. *Journal of the American Psychoanalytic Association* 40(4): 955–89.

Isay, R. A. 1989. *Being Homosexual.* New York: Farrar, Straus, and Giroux.

Josselyn, I. 1971. The capacity to love: A possible reformulation. *Journal of the American Academy of Child Psychiatry.*

Kernberg, O. F. 1974. Mature love: Prerequisites and characteristics. *Journal of the American Psychoanalytic Association* 22:743–68.

———. 1991. Sadomasochism, sexual excitement, and perversion. *Journal of the American Psychoanalytic Association* 39(2): 333–62.

———. 1993. *Aggression in Personality Disorders and Perversion.* New Haven: Yale University Press.

Kohut, H. 1971. *The Analysis of the Self.* New York: International Universities Press.

———. 1973. Thoughts on narcissism and narcissistic rage. In *The Psychoanalytic Study of the Child* 27:360–400. New Haven: Yale University Press.

———. 1977. *The Restoration of the Self.* New York: International Universities Press.

———. 1984. *How Does Analysis Cure?* Chicago: University of Chicago Press.

Kohut, H., and Seitz, P. 1963. Concepts and theories of psychoanalysis. In *Concepts of Personality,* ed. J. Wepman and R. Heine. Chicago: Aldine.

LaPlanche, J., and Pontalis, J. B. 1973. *The Language of Psychoanalysis.* New York: W. W. Norton.

Leavy, Stanley. Toward a further understanding of homosexual men. *Journal of the American Psychoanalytic Association* 34(1): 193–206.

Lever, M. 1993. *Sade: A Biography.* New York: Putnam.

Levine, M. 1952. Principles of psychiatric treatment. In *Dynamic Psychiatry,* ed. F. Alexander and H. Ross. Chicago: University of Chicago Press.

Lewis, M., Stanger, C., and Sullivan, M. N. 1989. Deception in three-year-olds. *Developmental Psychology* 25:439–43.

McDougall, J. 1978. *Plea for a Measure of Abnormality*. New York: International Universities Press.

Manfield, P. 1993. *Split Self/Split Object*. Northvale, N.J.: Jason Aronson.

Meares, R. 1993. *The Metaphor of Play*. Northvale, N.J.: Jason Aronson.

Moore, B. E., and Fine, B. D., eds. 1983. *Psychoanalytic Terms and Concepts*. New Haven: Yale University Press.

Morgenthaler, F. 1980. *Homosexuality, Heterosexuality, Perversion*. Hillsdale, N.J.: Analytic Press.

Rudden, M., Sweeney, J., and Francis, A. 1990. Diagnosis and clinical course of erotomania and other delusional patients. *American Journal of Psychiatry* 147(5): 125–38.

Schwaber, E. 1992. Psychoanalytic theory and its relation to clinical work. *Journal of the American Psychoanalytic Association* 40(4): 1039–57.

Segal, J. 1989. Erotomania revisited: From Kraepelin to DSM III-R. *American Journal of Psychiatry* 146(10): 1261–66.

Socarides, C. 1992. Sexual politics and scientific logic: The issue of homosexuality. *Journal of Psychohistory* 10(3).

Steiner, R. 1989. On narcissism: The Kleinian approach. In *The Psychiatric Clinics of North America Narcissistic Personality Disorder*, ed. O. Kernberg. Philadelphia: W. B. Saunders.

Stoller, R. J. 1975. *Perversion: The Erotic Form of Hatred*. New York: Pantheon.

———. 1991. Eros and Polis: What is this thing called love? *Journal of the American Psychoanalytic Association* 39(4): 1065–1102.

Stolorow, R. 1975. The narcissistic function of masochism (and sadism). *International Journal of Psycho-analysis* 56:441–48.

Stolorow, R., and Trop, J. L. 1993. Reply to Blochner, Lesser, and Schwartz, *Psychoanalytic Dialogues* 3(4): 653.

Winnicott, D. W. 1960. Ego distinction in terms of true and false self. *The Maturational Processes and the Facilitating Environment*. New York: International Universities Press, 1965.

Index